More Practice in Mathematics
New Edition

J. W. Adams and R. P. Beaumont
Edited by T. R. Goddard

© **1982 Schofield & Sims Ltd**

All rights reserved.
No part of this publication may be reproduced,
stored in a retrieval system, or transmitted,
in any form, or by any means, electronic,
mechanical, photocopying, recording or otherwise,
without the prior permission of Schofield & Sims Ltd.

0 7217 2348 9

First printed 1982
Revised and reprinted 1984
Reprinted 1986

More Practice is a series of five books.
Book 1	0 7217 2346 2	Answers 1	0 7217 2351 9
Book 2	0 7217 2347 0	Answers 2	0 7217 2352 7
Book 3	0 7217 2348 9	Answers 3	0 7217 2353 5
Book 4	0 7217 2349 7	Answers 4	0 7217 2354 3
Book 5	0 7217 2350 0	Answers 5	0 7217 2355 1

Schofield & Sims Ltd   Huddersfield

Contents

UNIT				page
1	Number to 1000	notation	place value	4,
2	Money	counting coins		6,
3	Addition and subtraction	number facts	money	8,
4	Number and money	+, − practice		10, 1
5	Time	12-hour clock		12, 1
6	Multiplication and division	number facts		14, 1
7	Number and money	×, ÷ practice		16, 1
8	Graphs			18, 1
9	Fractions			20, 2
10	Length	mm cm		22, 2
11	Length	mm cm m km		24, 2
12	**Looking back**			26, 2
13	Decimal fractions	notation, tenths		28, 2
14	Mass	grams kilograms		30, 3
15	Capacity	millilitres litres		32, 3
16	Number, money, measures	+, −		34, 3
17	Time	24-hour clock	The calendar	36, 3
18	Lines and angles			38, 3
19	**Looking back**			40, 4
20	Decimal fractions	notation, tenths, hundredths		42, 4
21	Decimal fractions	notation, tenths, hundredths		44, 4
22	Number, money, measures	×, ÷		46, 4
23	Shapes	quadrilaterals		48, 4
24	Plans	drawing to scale		50, 5
25	Shopping	costing items		52, 5
26	**Looking back**			54, 5
27	Shapes	triangles		56, 5
28	Number and money	four rules		58, 5
29	Area	squares, rectangles		60, 6
30	Area	squares, rectangles, irregular shapes		62, 6
31	Shapes	circles		64, 6
32	Solids	cubes, cuboids—volume		66, 6
33, 34	**Looking back**			68–7

Topics

		UNIT
Number: money		
Notation	Th H T U	1
	Decimal fractions—	
	tenths	13
	tenths, hundredths	20, 21
Addition and subtraction	Number facts	3
	Graded practice	4
	Practice	16, 28
Multiplication and division	Number facts	6
	Graded practice	7
	Practice	22, 28
Shopping	Counting coins Change	2
	Costing items	22, 25
Miscellaneous practice	Multiples, factors, prime numbers	6
	Square numbers	12
Fractions	Vulgar Decimal, tenths	9, 13
Measures		
Length	mm cm	10
	mm cm m km	11
	perimeter	10, 11, 23, 30
Mass	g kg dials and scales	14
Capacity	mℓ litre reading scales	15
Miscellaneous practice		16, 22
Shopping	Costing items	22, 25
Time	12-hour clock Telling the time	5
	Time, speed and distance	5
	24-hour clock	17
	The calendar Time line	17
Graphs	Block, line	8
Lines	Vertical, horizontal, oblique	18
	Parallel, perpendicular	18
Angles	Acute, obtuse, right angles	18, 23
	Compass points Direction	18
Shapes	Quadrilaterals sides, angles	23
	construction	23
	Triangles sides, angles	27
	construction	27
	Circles	31
Plans	Scale drawings	11, 24
Area	Squares, rectangles cm^2	29, 30
	Irregular shapes	30
Volume	Solids cubes, cuboids, cm^3	32
Looking back	Revision	12, 19, 26, 33, 34

UNIT 1
Number to 1000 notation place value

A
1 Write the number shown on each abacus picture in figures and in words.

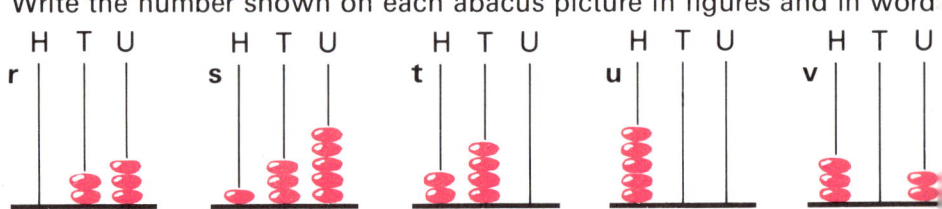

Draw an abacus picture to show 2 7 more than abacus picture **r**
3 5 more than **s** 4 60 more than **t** 5 300 more than **u** 6 98 more than **v**

Write and complete.
7 376 = ☐hundreds ☐tens ☐units = ☐tens ☐units
8 580 = ☐hundreds ☐tens ☐units = ☐tens ☐units
9 704 = ☐hundreds ☐tens ☐units = ☐tens ☐units
10 400 = ☐hundreds = ☐tens = ☐units

B
1 20 + 30   2 50 + 40   3 30 + 60   4 80 + 2
5 70 + 40   6 30 + 90   7 80 + 50   8 190 + 1
9 70 − 20   10 90 − 70   11 80 − 30   12 100 − 6
13 120 − 50 14 110 − 60 15 160 − 80 16 130 − 7

C
1 Write the number shown on each abacus picture in figures and in words.

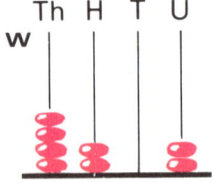 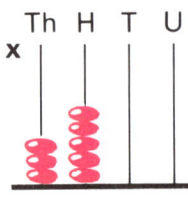 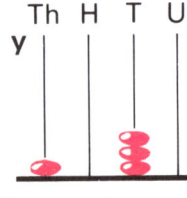 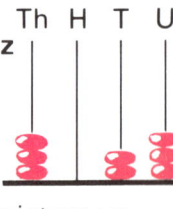

Draw an abacus picture to show 2 8 more than abacus picture **w**
3 500 more than **x**   4 70 more than **y**   5 77 more than **z**

Write and complete.
6 3450 = ☐thousands ☐hundreds ☐tens ☐units
       = ☐hundreds ☐tens ☐units = ☐tens ☐units
7 2900 = ☐thousands ☐hundreds ☐tens ☐units
       = ☐hundreds ☐tens ☐units = ☐tens ☐units
8 1080 = ☐thousand ☐hundreds ☐tens ☐units
       = ☐hundreds ☐tens ☐units = ☐tens ☐units
9 Draw four columns and write these numbers in order, the largest first.
   three thousand
   three hundred and three
   three hundred and thirty-three
   three thousand three hundred
   three hundred and thirty

D Write in figures and in words the value of each figure underlined.
1 4015   2 37<u>0</u>8   3 9<u>3</u>60   4 561<u>7</u>   5 22<u>2</u>2

Rearrange the digits below to make the largest possible whole number.
6 0, 1, 6, 8   7 2, 1, 0, 8   8 0, 4, 1, 0

Write the answers only.
9 3000 + 400 + 50 + 5   10 2000 + 80 + 9   11 1000 + 500
12 5000 + 200 + 70   13 6000 + 600 + 6   14 9000 + 9
15 200 + 30 + 8000   16 20 + 2000 + 200   17 6 + 90 + 3000

Find each missing number.
18 4000 + ☐ + 9 = 4069   19 3000 + 500 + ☐ + 6 = 3586
20 1000 + ☐ + 70 + 1 = 1271   21 7000 + 100 + ☐ + 1 = 7111

E

W	X	Y	Z
4	4	4	4

In this number, each digit has been named with a letter.

How many times **larger** is
1 the digit marked Y than that marked Z   2 X than Z
3 W than Z   4 X than Y   5 W than Y   6 W than X?

How many times **smaller** is the digit marked
7 Z than Y   8 Z than X   9 Z than W   10 Y than X
11 Y than W   12 X than W?

F Multiply by 10. Write the answers only.
1 9   2 90   3 900   4 16   5 43
6 11   7 250   8 475   9 171   10 609

Divide by 10. Write the answers only.
11 20   12 200   13 2000   14 180   15 310
16 770   17 4600   18 5440   19 8250   20 9030

G Multiply by 100. Write the answers only.
1 5   2 10   3 30   4 60   5 80
6 17   7 45   8 53   9 72   10 99

Divide by 100. Write the answers only.
11 200   12 900   13 5000   14 7000   15 4000
16 1900   17 2100   18 6600   19 8200   20 3400

Write the largest even number that can be made by rearranging these digits.
21 2, 3, 4, 7   22 2, 4, 3, 0   23 1, 9, 2, 7

Write the smallest odd number that can be made by rearranging these digits.
24 2, 1, 8, 7   25 5, 4, 2, 3   26 1, 6, 8, 5

UNIT 2
Money counting coins

A Write and complete.
1. £1 = ☐FIFTIES = ☐TWENTIES = ☐TENS = ☐FIVES = ☐TWOS
2. 1 FIFTY = ☐TENS = ☐FIVES = ☐TWOS
3. 1 TWENTY = ☐TENS = ☐FIVES = ☐TWOS

How many FIFTIES for   4 £3   5 £4   6 £5   7 £10
How many TWENTIES for 8 £2   9 £3   10 £5 11 £10
How many TENS for   12 £2 13 £3 14 £5 15 £10
How many FIVES for   16 £2 17 £3 18 £4 19 £5?

B How many TWENTIES have the same value as
1 20 TWOS   2 30 TWOS   3 8 FIVES   4 40 FIVES
5 6 TENS   6 14 TENS   7 18 TENS   8 24 TENS?

How many TENS have the same value as
9 80p   10 130p   11 15 TWOS 12 40 TWOS
13 8 FIVES 14 14 FIVES 15 24 FIVES 16 30 FIVES

How many FIVES have the same value as
17 25p   18 45p   19 55p   20 75p
21 10 TWOS 22 15 TWOS 23 35 TWOS 24 60 TWOS

How much change from a FIFTY after spending
25 8p   26 22p   27 17p   28 26p   29 35p
30 23p   31 19p   32 11p   33 24p   34 38p?

How much change from £1 after spending
35 75p   36 37p   37 69p   38 84p   39 63p
40 56p   41 42p   42 77p   43 52p   44 21p

C Look at the coins in the box.

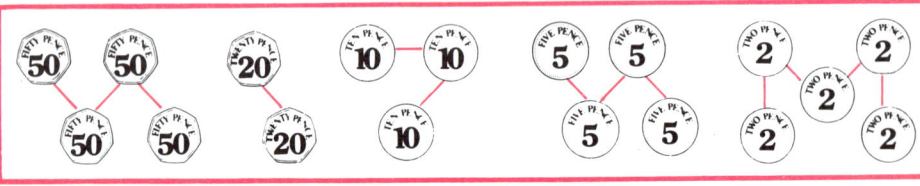

How many
1 £s are equal in value to the FIFTIES
2 TWENTIES are equal in value to the TENS, FIVES and TWOS together?
3 Find the total value of the coins in £s.

Find the total value of the coins in each box below.

Which three coins together make these amounts?
6 17p   7 56p   8 23p   9 8p
10 31p   11 14p   12 41p   13 90

6

D

1. Write as £s the total amount each child has saved.
2. How much less than £1 has each child saved? Write each answer as pence.

	50	20	10	5	2	1
Tony	1	1	1	3	2	
Peter		3	2		4	5
Jane	1		1	4	3	6
Mary		2	1	5	6	

Write each of these amounts as £s.

3. 57p   4. 24p   5. 9p   6. 128p   7. 367p
8. 408p   9. 210p   10. 450p   11. 307p   12. 200p

How many pennies have the same value as

13. £0·34   14. £0·06   15. £2·07   16. £8·50   17. £6·51
18. £0·10   19. £0·92   20. £3·24   21. £5·08   22. £9·00?

£5·50   £0·55   £5·55   £5·05   £0·50

23. Write the prices above in order. Put the largest first.
24. Take the smallest amount from the largest.

E Write each of these amounts as £s.

1. 30 TWOS   2. 45 TWOS   3. 54 TWOS   4. 80 TWOS
5. 17 FIVES   6. 23 FIVES   7. 50 FIVES   8. 75 FIVES
9. 7 TENS   10. 11 TENS   11. 67 TENS   12. 94 TENS
13. 7 TWENTIES   14. 8 TWENTIES   15. 10 TWENTIES   16. 35 TWENTIES

17. Draw and complete this table.

Use the least number of coins to make up each amount.

The first one is done for you.

amount	50	20	10	5	2	1
95p	1	2		1		
38p						
67p						
29p						

18. Now write these sums of money in your table and write the coins, using the least number, to make up each amount.
£0·35   £0·83   £0·92   £0·79   £0·44

F How many FIVES are equal in value to

1. £0·55   2. £0·90   3. £1·25   4. £1·50   5. £2·30?

How many TENS are equal in value to

6. £1·80   7. £2·30   8. £3·90   9. £4·60   10. £6·50?

How many TWENTIES are equal in value to

11. £1·40   12. £2·20   13. £4·80   14. £7·60   15. £9·40?

How many FIFTIES are equal in value to

16. £2·50   17. £5·50   18. £7·50   19. £9·50   20. £12·00?

7

UNIT 3

Addition and subtraction
number facts   money

A Write the answers only.
1. 9 + 2
2. 4 + 7
3. 6 + 5
4. 8 + 9
5. 3 + 9
6. 7 + 8
7. 8 + 5
8. 9 + 7
9. 5 + 7
10. 8 + 4
11. 6 + 9
12. 3 + 8
13. 7 + 4
14. 9 + 5
15. 6 + 6
16. 8 + 7
17. 9 + 4
18. 6 + 8
19. 4 + 8
20. 7 + 6
21. 9 + 9
22. 5 + 8
23. 7 + 7
24. 9 + 6
25. 8 + 8
26. 4 + 9
27. 8 + 3
28. 5 + 9
29. 7 + 9
30. 9 + 3
31. 7 + 5
32. 9 + 8
33. 8 + 6
34. 5 + 6
35. 6 + 7

B Write the answers only.
1. 14 − 5
2. 11 − 9
3. 12 − 4
4. 15 − 7
5. 18 − 9
6. 11 − 8
7. 14 − 8
8. 17 − 9
9. 14 − 6
10. 13 − 7
11. 15 − 9
12. 12 − 3
13. 11 − 7
14. 16 − 8
15. 11 − 5
16. 12 − 8
17. 12 − 6
18. 13 − 9
19. 11 − 4
20. 15 − 6
21. 13 − 5
22. 17 − 8
23. 12 − 5
24. 14 − 7
25. 16 − 9
26. 12 − 7
27. 13 − 6
28. 14 − 9
29. 13 − 8
30. 11 − 3
31. 13 − 4
32. 15 − 8
33. 16 − 7
34. 11 − 6
35. 12 − 9

C Find the value of y.
1. $3 + y = 12$
2. $y + 8 = 14$
3. $2 + y = 11$
4. $y + 8 = 12$
5. $6 + y = 11$
6. $y + 7 = 13$
7. $8 + y = 15$
8. $y + 9 = 14$
9. $5 + y = 13$
10. $y + 6 = 15$
11. $6 + y = 12$
12. $y + 4 = 11$
13. $8 + y = 17$
14. $y + 7 = 14$
15. $4 + y = 13$
16. $y + 5 = 14$
17. $7 + y = 12$
18. $y + 3 = 11$
19. $9 + y = 18$
20. $y + 8 = 16$
21. $9 + y = 15$
22. $y + 4 = 12$
23. $7 + y = 16$
24. $y + 6 = 13$

D Find the value of z.
1. $18 − z = 9$
2. $z − 6 = 8$
3. $13 − z = 4$
4. $z − 9 = 8$
5. $13 − z = 6$
6. $z − 9 = 5$
7. $17 − z = 9$
8. $z − 5 = 8$
9. $11 − z = 8$
10. $z − 7 = 4$
11. $14 − z = 7$
12. $z − 9 = 3$
13. $16 − z = 7$
14. $z − 4 = 8$
15. $14 − z = 6$
16. $z − 7 = 8$
17. $11 − z = 3$
18. $z − 6 = 9$
19. $16 − z = 8$
20. $z − 7 = 5$
21. $15 − z = 6$
22. $z − 9 = 2$
23. $16 − z = 9$
24. $z − 5 = 6$

E Find the sum of
1. 9 and 7
2. 8 and 5
3. 9 and 3.

Take
4. 4 from 13
5. 8 from 17
6. 9 from 18

7. What number is 5 greater than 6?

Find the difference between
8. 12 and 7
9. 15 and 8.

Find the total of
10. 3 and 9
11. 5 and 7
12. 6 and 8.

Subtract
13. 5 from 14
14. 6 from 13
15. 4 from 11

F Bridging the tens.
1 9 + 2   2 19 + 2   3 29 + 2   4 39 + 2   5 69 + 2
6 4 + 18 7 4 + 28   8 4 + 38   9 4 + 48   10 4 + 78
11 26 + 5 12 36 + 5   13 46 + 5   14 66 + 5   15 86 + 5
16 7 + 14 17 7 + 24   18 7 + 34   19 7 + 54   20 7 + 74
21 33 + 8 22 43 + 8   23 53 + 8   24 73 + 8   25 93 + 8

G Write the answers only.
1 11 − 2 2 21 − 2   3 31 − 2   4 41 − 2   5 71 − 2
6 14 − 7 7 24 − 7   8 34 − 7   9 44 − 7   10 84 − 7
11 13 − 5 12 23 − 5   13 33 − 5   14 63 − 5   15 93 − 5
16 22 − 4 17 32 − 4   18 42 − 4   19 72 − 4   20 82 − 4
21 16 − 8 22 26 − 8   23 36 − 8   24 66 − 8   25 96 − 8

H Find the value of **p**.
1 8 + 3 = 5 + p   2 6 + 7 = 4 + p   3 9 + 5 = 7 + p
4 9 + 2 = p + 7   5 8 + 8 = p + 9   6 7 + 6 = p + 5
7 4 + p = 6 + 6   8 5 + p = 9 + 3   9 9 + p = 7 + 8
10 p + 8 = 9 + 7   11 p + 6 = 5 + 9   12 p + 7 = 6 + 9

Find the value of **t**.
13 11 − 5 = 13 − t   14 16 − 9 = 14 − t   15 13 − 4 = 17 − t
16 14 − 8 = t − 6   17 11 − 8 = t − 9   18 17 − 9 = t − 6
19 12 − t = 13 − 8   20 15 − t = 11 − 4   21 12 − t = 15 − 6
22 t − 5 = 15 − 9   23 t − 8 = 12 − 4   24 t − 8 = 14 − 9

Write the answers only.
1 (1 + 9) + 4   2 9 + (5 + 5)   3 (7 + 3) + 2   4 8 + 6 + 2
5 (6 + 4) + 7   6 5 + (8 + 2)   7 3 + (9 + 1)   8 5 + 8 + 5
9 (2 + 8) + 6   10 4 + (3 + 7)   11 (5 + 5) + 2   12 9 + 7 + 1
13 (7 + 3) + 5   14 6 + (1 + 9)   15 9 + (4 + 6)   16 6 + 5 + 4
17 (5 + 5) + 3   18 2 + (6 + 4)   19 (8 + 2) + 7   20 3 + 8 + 7

1 15 − 3 − 8   2 18 − 4 − 9   3 13 − 2 − 6   4 17 − 4 − 5
5 16 − 4 − 6   6 15 − 2 − 7   7 14 − 3 − 9   8 18 − 3 − 9
9 11 − 4 − 2   10 14 − 6 − 3   11 16 − 9 − 5   12 17 − 8 − 6
13 13 − 8 − 5   14 12 − 3 − 4   15 15 − 8 − 4   16 16 − 7 − 8
17 18 − 9 − 4   18 17 − 9 − 5   19 14 − 7 − 3   20 11 − 3 − 2

K
1 What must be added to a FIVE and a TWO to make 15p?
  Increase   2 3p by 7p   3 7p by 7p   4 9p by 7p.
  Decrease   5 15p by 8p   6 13p by 6p.
7 Find the total in pence of 1 FIVE, 3 TWOS and 7 pence.
8 Tom spent 6p and 7p. How much change had he from a TWENTY?

UNIT 4

Number and money
addition and subtraction graded practice

Work **Section A**. Mark the answers and correct any mistakes.
Do the same with Sections B and C.

A 1
```
   205
    42
+  532
```
2
```
     1
    54
+  630
```
3
```
   402
    15
+ 1463
```
4
```
   530
    16
+    ?
```
5
```
  2093
   114
+  702
```
6
```
  1568
  3101
+ 1240
```
7
```
    32
  3060
+  708
```
8
```
   460
   10?
+  22?
```

B 1
```
    £
 3·15
 0·24
 2·06
+0·03
```
2
```
    £
 2·48
 0·16
 0·22
+3·03
```
3
```
    £
 0·09
 6·14
 3·22
+0·41
```
4
```
    £
 2·1
 1·3
 2·1
+4·?
```
5
```
    £
 0·39
 0·27
 4·16
+5·03
```
6
```
    £
 2·15
 1·07
 0·08
+3·64
```
7
```
    £
 2·18
12·04
 1·35
+23·26
```
8
```
    £
 1·1
 2·?
32·?
+10·0
```

C 1
```
   38
   50
  429
+  52
```
2
```
  310
  196
   48
+ 156
```
3
```
  489
 1174
  126
+3015
```
4
```
  21?
  10?
   2?
+  4?
```
5
```
    £
 1·96
24·34
 2·79
+10·25
```
6
```
    £
 2·33
45·65
10·04
+15·72
```
7
```
    £
 0·98
34·37
21·59
+16·36
```
8
```
    £
14·
18·
 0·
+26·
```

D The table shows the weekly attendance at four schools during February.
Find the total attendance at the four schools for the week ending

school	week ending			
	Feb. 4	Feb. 11	Feb. 18	Feb. 2
Northdown	994	1065	1019	1097
Howsell	1236	1198	1177	1206
Lorden	954	870	936	984
Tranton	767	801	835	790

1 4th Feb.   2 11th Feb.
3 18th Feb.   4 25th Feb.
5 What is the grand total attendance for the four schools?
Find the total attendance for the four weeks at these schools.
6 Northdown   7 Howsell   8 Lorden   9 Trant
10 Find the grand total attendance for the four weeks.
11 The grand total attendance has been found in two ways.
Are both totals the same? If not work questions 1 to 10 again.

E 1) 478   2) 963   3) 2815   4) 3496
      − 253   − 750   − 1713   − 2103

   5) £   6) £   7) £   8) £
       5·78   6·75   36·42   80·65
     − 4·30   − 6·02   − 10·02   − 50·40

F 1) 470   2) 1380   3) 2709   4) 5056
      − 342   − 255   − 1148   − 1732

   5) £   6) £   7) £   8) £
       9·08   3·07   40·95   60·00
     − 3·64   − 0·82   − 3·63   − 43·11

G 1) 945   2) 567   3) 1600   4) 3843
      − 186   − 79   − 1266   − 3747

   5) £   6) £   7) £   8) £
       8·32   19·51   31·27   45·67
     − 2·06   − 5·44   − 30·18   − 25·70

H 1) 500   2) 2056   3) 2830   4) 7135
      − 41   − 79   − 1990   − 857

   5) £   6) £   7) £   8) £
       8·94   6·05   26·52   47·61
     − 4·08   − 3·02   − 0·59   − 27·07

1) Make a list of all the items for sale below.
2) By the side of each, write the amount of the reduction from the old price to the sale price.

BROWN'S CHILDREN'S TOY DEPARTMENT

SPECIAL SALE

GREAT REDUCTIONS

	Old Price	Sale Price		Old Price	Sale Price
Cars	£20·00	£18·75	Microscopes	£17·50	£16·55
Swings	£19·86	£18·95	Typewriters	£23·42	£20·60
Tricycles	£15·68	£13·99	Record Players	£27·99	£26·76
Scooters	£10·00	£8·50	Tape Recorders	£29·77	£27·80
Go-Karts	£34·34	£32·78	Radios	£17·00	£15·51

11

UNIT 5

Time 12-hour clock

A

1 Write the time shown on each clock face—first in figures and then in words.

before noon

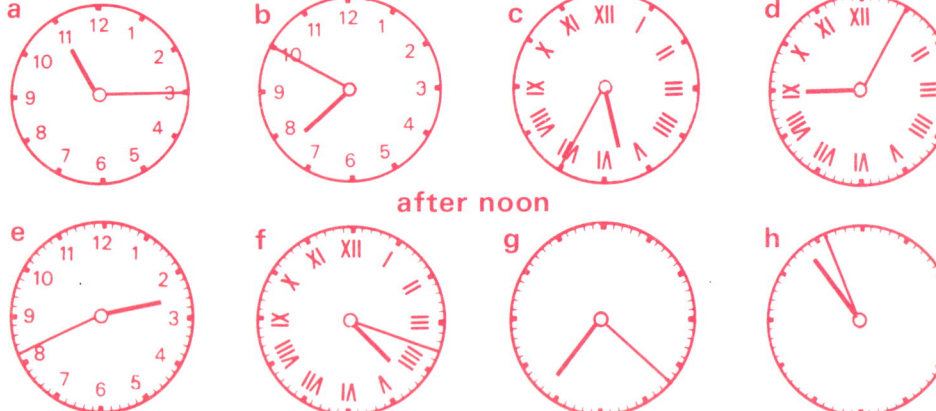

after noon

Write in figures, using a.m. or p.m., the correct time if

2 clock **a** is $\frac{1}{2}$ hour slow
3 clock **b** is $\frac{1}{4}$ hour fast
4 clock **c** is 25 min slow
5 clock **d** is 5 min fast
6 clock **e** is 20 min slow
7 clock **f** is 19 min fast
8 clock **g** is 13 min slow
9 clock **h** is $\frac{1}{2}$ hour fast.

B The diagram shows a circular bus route from **Kenton** and the times the bus arrives at different villages.

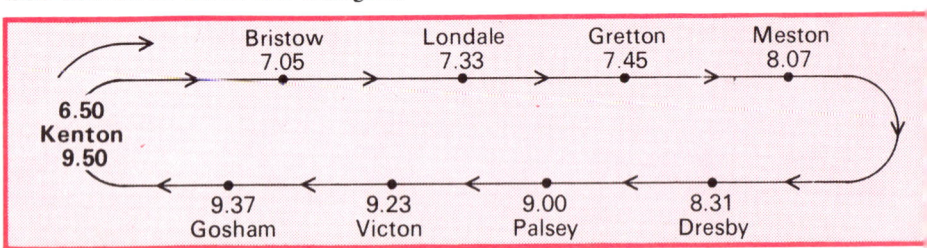

How long does the bus take from

1 **Kenton** to Bristow
2 Bristow to Londale
3 Londale to Gretton
4 Gretton to Meston
5 Meston to Dresby
6 Dresby to Palsey
7 Palsey to Victon
8 Victon to Gosham
9 Gosham to **Kenton**

How long does it take to travel from

10 Londale to Palsey
11 Bristow to Gosham
12 Gretton to Victon
13 Meston to Kenton?

C How many hours (h) and minutes (min) is it from

1 10.35 a.m. to noon
2 9.50 a.m. to noon
3 8.37 a.m. to noon
4 6.30 a.m. to noon
5 7.19 a.m. to noon
6 10.04 a.m. to noon
7 noon to 12.45 p.m.
8 noon to 1.15 p.m.
9 noon to 2.10 p.m.
10 noon to 3.38 p.m.
11 noon to 4.02 p.m.
12 noon to 5.50 p.m.
13 11.30 a.m. to 12.40 p.m.
14 11.40 a.m. to 12.55 p.m.
15 10.51 a.m. to 12.18 p.m.
16 11.24 a.m. to 1.10 p.m.?

D

1 Write in words the time shown on each of these digital clocks.

W 12 00   X 10 35   Y 05 15   Z 01 50

2 Write the time in figures as it would have been shown on each digital clock 2½ hours earlier.

How many minutes in

3 1½ h   4 2 h   5 1 h 40 min   6 1 h 55 min
7 4 h   8 3¾ h   9 2 h 37 min   10 5¼ h?

Change to hours and minutes.

11 75 min   12 98 min   13 110 min   14 137 min
15 150 min   16 180 min   17 200 min   18 250 min

How many seconds in

19 1 min   20 ½ min   21 ¼ min   22 1¾ min
23 2 min   24 2¼ min   25 3 min   26 5 min?

How many hours from

27 midnight to noon   28 noon to midnight   29 noon to noon
30 7 a.m. to 7 p.m.   31 9 a.m. to 8 p.m.   32 10 a.m. to 6 p.m.
33 6 p.m. to 1 a.m.   34 8 p.m. to 3 a.m.   35 5 p.m. to 4 a.m.?

How many hours in

36 1 day   37 4 days   38 5 days   39 1 week?

E

For each of the following, four times are given. Choose the time which you think is the most suitable.

1	To run 100 metres	20 s	2 min	80 s	8 min
2	To boil an egg	50 s	1 min	10 s	4 min
3	To count to 100	1 min	10 s	3 min	5 min
4	To write the alphabet	3½ min	7 min	½ min	9½ min
5	To eat your dinner	1 hour	¾ hour	75 min	⅓ hour

The car takes 15 s to make one lap of the track.

6 Copy and complete the table below.

time in minutes and seconds	0 min 15 s							
number of laps	1	2	3	4	6	8	10

F

Find the value of the missing number in each example.

	time	speed	distance
1	2 h	10 km/h	☐ km
2	3 h	15 km/h	☐ km
3	5 h	☐ km/h	100 km
4	10 h	☐ km/h	500 km

	time	speed	distance
5	☐ h	20 km/h	40 km
6	☐ h	50 km/h	150 km
7	4 h	35 km/h	☐ km
8	7 h	☐ km/h	140 km

13

UNIT 6

Multiplication and division
number facts

A Copy and complete the following **multiples of 2, 4 and 8**.
1 Multiples of 2.   2, 4, 6, ☐, ☐, ☐, ☐, ☐, ☐, 20
2 Multiples of 4.   4, 8, ☐, ☐, ☐, ☐, ☐, ☐, ☐, 40
3 Multiples of 8.   8, ☐, ☐, ☐, ☐, ☐, ☐, ☐, ☐, 80

| 5, | 9, | 0, | 3, | 6, | 8, | 4, | 7 |

Multiply each of the numbers above
4 by 2   5 by 4   6 by 8.

B Copy and complete the following **multiples of 3, 6 and 9**.
1 Multiples of 3.   3, 6, ☐, ☐, ☐, ☐, ☐, ☐, ☐, 30
2 Multiples of 6.   6, ☐, ☐, ☐, ☐, ☐, ☐, ☐, ☐, 60
3 Multiples of 9.   9, ☐, ☐, ☐, ☐, ☐, ☐, ☐, ☐, 90

| 8, | 3, | 9, | 4, | 7, | 5, | 6, | 0 |

Multiply each of the numbers above
4 by 3   5 by 6   6 by 9.

C Copy and complete the following **multiples of 5, 7 and 10**.
1 Multiples of 5.   5, ☐, ☐, ☐, ☐, ☐, ☐, ☐, ☐, 50
2 Multiples of 7.   7, ☐, ☐, ☐, ☐, ☐, ☐, ☐, ☐, 70
3 Multiples of 10. 10, ☐, ☐, ☐, ☐, ☐, ☐, ☐, ☐, 100

| 3, | 0, | 7, | 4, | 6, | 9, | 5, | 8 |

Multiply each of the numbers above
4 by 5   5 by 7   6 by 10.

D Write the answers only.
1 $(3 \times 4) + 2$ 2 $(6 \times 4) + 5$ 3 $(8 \times 8) + 4$ 4 $(9 \times 4) + 3$
5 $(4 \times 8) + 3$ 6 $(9 \times 9) + 8$ 7 $(6 \times 2) + 2$ 8 $(7 \times 6) + 6$
9 $(7 \times 2) + 6$ 10 $(7 \times 8) + 4$ 11 $(8 \times 9) + 7$ 12 $(6 \times 3) + 2$
13 $(4 \times 7) + 2$ 14 $(6 \times 9) + 5$ 15 $(6 \times 6) + 4$ 16 $(9 \times 7) + 7$
17 $(8 \times 3) + 7$ 18 $(7 \times 7) + 5$ 19 $(9 \times 5) + 8$ 20 $(8 \times 6) + 3$
21 $(9 \times 2) + 6$ 22 $(9 \times 3) + 8$ 23 $(7 \times 5) + 6$ 24 $(8 \times 2) + 3$

E A number which will divide **exactly** into another number is a **factor** of that number, e.g. 1, 2, 4 and 8 are all factors of 8.

| 1, | 2, | 3, | 4, | 5, | 6, | 7, | 8, | 9, | 10 |

Which of the numbers above are factors of
1 12   2 16   3 18   4 20   5 24   6 30

A **prime number** has only two factors—the number itself and 1, e.g. 5 is a prime number as it only has two factors, 5 and 1.

7 Write seven more prime numbers between 1 and 20.

F Write the answers only.

Divide by 2	**1** 20	**2** 14	**3** 8	**4** 16	**5** 6
	6 10	**7** 18	**8** 4	**9** 12	**10** 0
Divide by 4	**11** 12	**12** 8	**13** 32	**14** 4	**15** 16
	16 28	**17** 40	**18** 20	**19** 36	**20** 24
Divide by 8	**21** 40	**22** 64	**23** 0	**24** 56	**25** 16
	26 24	**27** 80	**28** 32	**29** 48	**30** 72

In the following, each answer includes a remainder.

31 2)¯13   **32** 4)¯19   **33** 8)¯60   **34** 4)¯27   **35** 8)¯29
36 4)¯22   **37** 8)¯43   **38** 2)¯19   **39** 4)¯31   **40** 8)¯53
41 2)¯17   **42** 4)¯39   **43** 8)¯79   **44** 4)¯35   **45** 8)¯69

G

Divide by 3	**1** 12	**2** 30	**3** 24	**4** 6	**5** 15
	6 9	**7** 18	**8** 3	**9** 21	**10** 27
Divide by 6	**11** 12	**12** 0	**13** 42	**14** 60	**15** 24
	16 36	**17** 54	**18** 18	**19** 48	**20** 30
Divide by 9	**21** 27	**22** 9	**23** 54	**24** 18	**25** 72
	26 63	**27** 81	**28** 36	**29** 90	**30** 45

In the following, each answer includes a remainder.

31 3)¯19   **32** 6)¯15   **33** 9)¯13   **34** 3)¯17   **35** 6)¯32
36 9)¯29   **37** 3)¯29   **38** 6)¯47   **39** 9)¯50   **40** 3)¯25
41 6)¯23   **42** 9)¯61   **43** 3)¯32   **44** 6)¯52   **45** 9)¯71

H

Divide by 5	**1** 20	**2** 35	**3** 45	**4** 10	**5** 0
	6 40	**7** 30	**8** 50	**9** 15	**10** 25
Divide by 7	**11** 42	**12** 7	**13** 56	**14** 14	**15** 35
	16 21	**17** 63	**18** 28	**19** 70	**20** 49
Divide by 10	**21** 80	**22** 30	**23** 50	**24** 70	**25** 90
	26 0	**27** 60	**28** 100	**29** 40	**30** 20

In the following, each answer includes a remainder.

31 5)¯17   **32** 7)¯24   **33** 10)¯22   **34** 5)¯33   **35** 7)¯39
36 10)¯34   **37** 5)¯48   **38** 7)¯53   **39** 10)¯58   **40** 5)¯29
41 7)¯61   **42** 10)¯77   **43** 5)¯36   **44** 7)¯68   **45** 10)¯99

I Write the answers only.
1 (4 × 5) + (7 × 7)   **2** (2 × 6) + (3 × 8)   **3** (3 × 10) + (1 × 9)
4 (5 × 8) − (6 × 4)   **5** (6 × 7) − (3 × 6)   **6** (10 × 9) − (7 × 8)
7 (28 ÷ 4) + (36 ÷ 6)   **8** (49 ÷ 7) + (25 ÷ 5)   **9** (72 ÷ 8) + (81 ÷ 9)
10 (54 ÷ 6) − (27 ÷ 9)   **11** (48 ÷ 6) − (35 ÷ 7)   **12** (100 ÷ 10) − (32 ÷ 4)

Write and complete using the sign × or ÷ instead of ●
13 (8 ● 5) = (4 ● 10)   **14** (4 ● 6) = (8 ● 3)   **15** (2 ● 8) = (4 ● 4)
16 (21 ● 3) = (14 ● 2)   **17** (45 ● 5) = (63 ● 7)   **18** (64 ● 8) = (32 ● 4)
19 (36 ● 4) = (3 ● 3)   **20** (4 ● 2) = (56 ● 7)   **21** (80 ● 8) = (2 ● 5)

15

UNIT 7

Number and money
multiplication and division practice

Work **Section A**. Mark the answers and correct any mistakes.
Do the same with Sections B and C.

A
| 1 | 60 × 2 | 2 | 190 × 3 | 3 | 180 × 4 | 4 | 160 × 5 |
| 5 | 207 × 6 | 6 | 308 × 8 | 7 | 404 × 9 | 8 | 506 × 7 |

Find the product of
9	34 and 2	10	13 and 3	11	22 and 4	12	21 and 5
13	2 and 28	14	3 and 43	15	4 and 46	16	5 and 37
17	27 and 6	18	48 and 7	19	19 and 8	20	33 and 9
21	6 and 46	22	7 and 29	23	8 and 56	24	9 and 82

B
1	119 × 5	2	223 × 4	3	115 × 6	4	328 × 3
5	151 × 9	6	382 × 4	7	271 × 7	8	393 × 3
9	478 × 8	10	395 × 6	11	467 × 9	12	384 × 5
13	965 × 5	14	563 × 7	15	269 × 9	16	276 × 8

C
1	£0·06 × 2	2	£0·05 × 6	3	£0·12 × 4	4	£0·11 × 8
5	£0·48 × 3	6	£0·39 × 7	7	£0·27 × 5	8	£0·63 × 9
9	£5·78 × 2	10	£4·94 × 5	11	£9·76 × 3	12	£6·48 × 4
13	£1·54 × 8	14	£2·58 × 9	15	£4·69 × 6	16	£3·48 × 7

D Find the answer to each of the following in two ways, first by addition, and then by multiplication.
1. 12 + 12 + 12 + 12 + 12 + 12
2. £0·63 + £0·63 + £0·63 + £0·63 + £0·63 + £0·63
3. 137 + 137 + 137 + 137 + 137
4. £3·49 + £3·49 + £3·49
5. £1·08 + £1·08 + £1·08 + £1·08

Work **Section E**. Mark the answers and correct any mistakes.
Do the same with Sections F, G and H.

1	2)156	2	3)273	3	9)486	4	4)312
5	6)3726	6	8)1248	7	5)2365	8	7)5299
9	4)720	10	3)2010	11	7)1680	12	9)5220
13	5)525	14	8)2456	15	6)5442	16	3)2127

1	5)944	2	4)751	3	7)963	4	6)893
5	3)4444	6	4)3794	7	8)4307	8	9)2676
9	5)2038	10	7)4240	11	6)1858	12	8)4070
13	3)812	14	9)5047	15	4)3043	16	6)3424
17	2)4081	18	7)7061	19	9)5402	20	5)9004

Money

Some of the following have remainders.

1	7)56p	2	8)72p	3	5)85p	4	6)96p
5	2)31p	6	4)38p	7	3)40p	8	9)85p

Write each answer in two ways—as £s and then as pence.

9	2)£0·98	10	5)£0·75	11	8)£2·56	12	6)£3·84
13	4)£0·56	14	3)£1·38	15	7)£3·85	16	9)£5·13

1	3)£9·06	2	8)£16·48	3	5)£20·45	4	6)£12·18
5	7)£16·10	6	3)£10·50	7	9)£16·20	8	4)£14·40
9	6)£13·44	10	5)£21·95	11	8)£30·88	12	3)£19·62
13	4)£27·04	14	9)£35·82	15	6)£21·12	16	7)£16·45
17	6)£12·18	18	8)£36·00	19	3)£6·03	20	5)£10·55
21	10)£24·30	22	10)£45·00	23	10)£30·50	24	10)£70·00

1 Find the value of the letter in each of the following.
   $8 \times a = 136$ $9 \times b = 261$ $7 \times c = 252$
   $6 \times d = £19·14$ $5 \times e = £41·50$ $4 \times f = £6·04$

The diagram shows how the children shared £36·24.

| Tim $\frac{1}{8}$ | Charles $\frac{1}{6}$ | Peter $\frac{1}{4}$ | Susan $\frac{1}{3}$ | John $\frac{1}{8}$ |

2 How much did each child receive?

UNIT 8
Graphs

A The number of persons who went on a visit to London is shown on the block graph.

Look at the horizontal and vertical axes of the graph.

1. On which axis are the numbers given?
2. How many divisions on the scale represent one person?
3. Name the axis on which men, women, etc. are shown.

men	
women	
boys	
girls	

4. Draw this table and find from the graph the number of each kind of person.
5. Find the total number of persons who went on the journey.

This chart shows the number of children who stayed at school for dinner

Mon.	Tues.	Wed.	Thurs.	Fri.
36	42	48	32	27

6. Draw a block graph. On the vertical axis show the number of children (let 1 division represent 1 child). On the horizontal axis show the days of the week.
7. Draw the graph again but this time let 1 division on the vertical scale represent 2 children. What difference does this make to the graph?
8. Find the total number of children.
9. Divide the total by the number of days to find the daily average.
10. Draw a dotted line on each graph to show the average.

B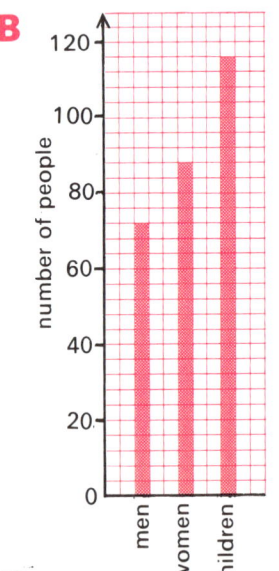

This block graph shows the number of people who travelled on a bus route.

What is shown on

1. the horizontal axis
2. the vertical axis?
3. What does one division on the vertical axis represent?

How many of the following travelled on the bus?

4. men
5. women
6. children

7. Draw a graph to show the following.
Let one division on the vertical axis represent 5 people.

men 75   women 110   children 160

On this graph, lines have been drawn instead of blocks. The graph shows a count of 100 children who spent different kinds of holidays.

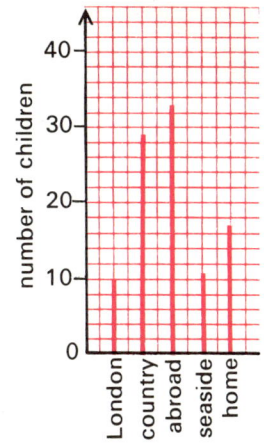

1. How many different kinds of holidays are given?
2. On which axis are they shown?
3. What information is given on the vertical axis?
4. What does each division represent?
5. How many children spent each kind of holiday? Write the answer in this way.
   Out of 100 children, ☐ went to London, ☐ went to the country, etc.
6. What fraction of the children spent each kind of holiday?

record of the count		total
to London	⧸⧸⧸⧸ ⧸⧸⧸⧸	
to the country	⧸⧸⧸⧸ ⧸⧸⧸⧸ ⧸⧸⧸⧸ ⧸⧸⧸⧸ ⧸	
to the seaside	⧸⧸⧸⧸ ⧸⧸⧸⧸ ⧸⧸⧸⧸ ⧸⧸⧸⧸ ⧸⧸⧸⧸ ⧸⧸⧸⧸ ⧸⧸⧸⧸ ⧸⧸⧸⧸ ⧸	
abroad	⧸⧸⧸⧸ ⧸⧸⧸⧸ ⧸⧸⧸⧸ ⧸⧸⧸⧸ ⧸⧸⧸⧸ ⧸⧸	
stayed at home	⧸⧸	

The record shows a count of another 100 children. A stroke (/) stands for **one child** and ⧸⧸⧸⧸ for **five children**.

7. Find the number of children who had each kind of holiday.
8. Draw a graph to show the result of the count.
9. Compare your graph with the one above. Write some of the differences you can see.

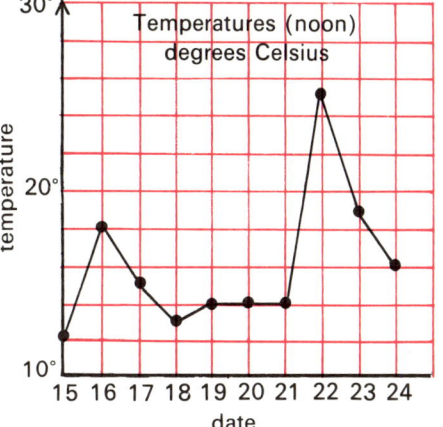

The graph shows the outside air temperature taken daily at noon. Each temperature is recorded by a dot and these are joined together by a thin line.

1. For how many days were the temperatures taken?
2. How many degrees are represented by one division on the vertical scale?

Between which dates was there
3. a rise   4. a fall in temperature?
5. On which dates did the temperature remain the same?
6. Read the temperature for each day and then find the average for the ten days.
7. During which of these months were the temperatures taken — February, July, December?

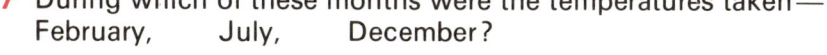
This table shows the temperatures at noon on each of 10 days.

date	22	23	24	25	26	27	28	29	30	31
temperature	0°	1°	8°	2°	4°	4°	2°	6°	3°	0°

8. Use this table to draw a graph and answer questions 3, 4, 5, 6 and 7 again.

UNIT 9
Fractions

A Strip W represents one whole one which has been divided into equal parts.

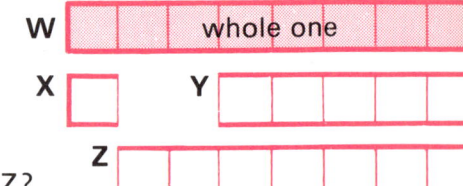

What fraction of strip W is
1 strip X   2 strip Y   3 strip Z ?

Each of the shapes below represents one whole one which has been divided into equal parts. Write the fraction of each shape which is shaded; is unshaded.

4 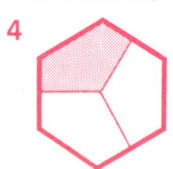   5 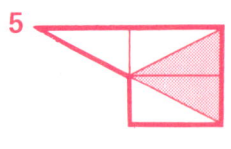   6    7 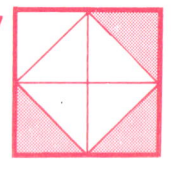   8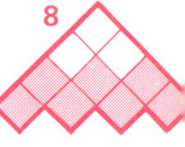

Write and complete.

9 $\frac{3}{5} + \frac{\Box}{5} = 1$ 10 $\frac{7}{8} + \frac{\Box}{8} = 1$ 11 $\frac{1}{10} + \frac{\Box}{10} = 1$ 12 $\frac{4}{7} + \frac{\Box}{7} = 1$

13 $\frac{5}{9} + \frac{\Box}{9} = 1$ 14 $\frac{7}{12} + \frac{\Box}{12} = 1$ 15 $1 - \frac{5}{6} = \frac{\Box}{6}$ 16 $1 - \frac{7}{12} = \frac{\Box}{12}$

17 $1 - \frac{5}{16} = \frac{\Box}{16}$ 18 $1 - \frac{1}{5} = \frac{\Box}{5}$ 19 $1 - \frac{3}{8} = \frac{\Box}{8}$ 20 $1 - \frac{7}{10} = \frac{\Box}{10}$

B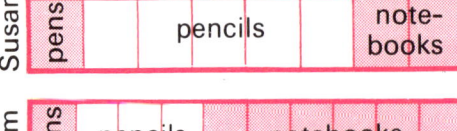

The diagrams show how each child spent £1·20 on pens, pencils and notebooks.

What **fraction** of the £1·20 did each child spend on
1 pens 2 pencils 3 notebooks

How much **money** did each child spend on
4 pens 5 pencils 6 notebooks

7 Count the number of sweets.

How many are there in   8 $\frac{1}{3}$ of the sweets   9 $\frac{2}{3}$ of the sweets

Find   10 $\frac{1}{3}$ of 18 biscuits   11 $\frac{2}{3}$ of 18 biscuits

12 $\frac{1}{4}$ of 28 apples   13 $\frac{3}{4}$ of 28 apples

14 $\frac{1}{6}$ of 24 sweets   15 $\frac{5}{6}$ of 24 sweets.

C Find   1 $\frac{1}{8}$ of 32p   2 $\frac{3}{8}$ of 32p   3 $\frac{5}{8}$ of 32p

4 $\frac{1}{5}$ of £50   5 $\frac{2}{5}$ of £50   6 $\frac{4}{5}$ of £50

7 $\frac{1}{7}$ of 21 m   8 $\frac{4}{7}$ of 21 m   9 $\frac{6}{7}$ of 21 m

10 $\frac{1}{10}$ of 100 g   11 $\frac{7}{10}$ of 100 g   12 $\frac{9}{10}$ of 100 g

13 $\frac{1}{100}$ of 1 km   14 $\frac{27}{100}$ of 1 km   15 $\frac{35}{100}$ of 1 km.

Find the whole number or quantity when

16 $\frac{1}{4}$ is 5p   17 $\frac{1}{8}$ is 6p   18 $\frac{1}{10}$ is 3p   19 $\frac{3}{4}$ is 12p

20 $\frac{5}{8}$ is 15p   21 $\frac{3}{10}$ is 27p   22 $\frac{5}{6}$ is 30 kg   23 $\frac{2}{3}$ is 10 litre

24 $\frac{7}{10}$ is 14 km   25 $\frac{4}{5}$ is £10   26 $\frac{9}{10}$ is 90 mℓ 27 $\frac{11}{100}$ is £33.

D Each of these strips represents a whole one.

Each whole one is divided into equal parts.

What fraction of the whole one, is one part of
1 strip **a** 2 strip **b** 3 strip **c**
4 strip **d** 5 strip **e** 6 strip **f**?

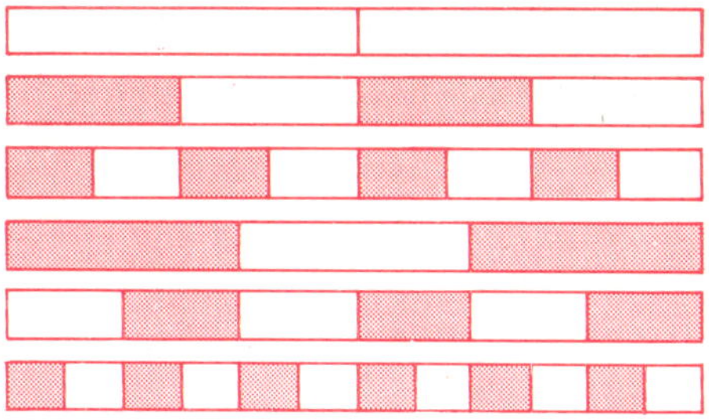

> greater than
< less than

Look at the strips above and then write and complete the following using > or < in place of ●

7 $\frac{1}{4}$ ● $\frac{1}{8}$ 8 $\frac{1}{3}$ ● $\frac{1}{6}$ 9 $\frac{1}{6}$ ● $\frac{1}{2}$ 10 $\frac{1}{6}$ ● $\frac{1}{4}$
11 $\frac{1}{3}$ ● $\frac{1}{8}$ 12 $\frac{1}{3}$ ● $\frac{1}{4}$ 13 $\frac{1}{12}$ ● $\frac{1}{2}$ 14 $\frac{1}{12}$ ● $\frac{1}{3}$
15 $\frac{1}{12}$ ● $\frac{1}{6}$ 16 $\frac{1}{2}$ ● $\frac{1}{3}$ 17 $\frac{1}{8}$ ● $\frac{1}{12}$ 18 $\frac{1}{8}$ ● $\frac{1}{6}$

19 Write these fractions in order of size, the largest first.
$\frac{1}{12}$, $\frac{1}{5}$, $\frac{1}{8}$, $\frac{1}{2}$, $\frac{1}{4}$, $\frac{1}{3}$, $\frac{1}{6}$

E Look at the strips above. Then write and complete.

1 $\frac{1}{2} = \frac{\Box}{4}$ 2 $\frac{1}{4} = \frac{\Box}{8}$ 3 $\frac{1}{2} = \frac{\Box}{6}$ 4 $\frac{1}{2} = \frac{\Box}{4} = \frac{\Box}{8}$
5 $\frac{1}{3} = \frac{\Box}{6} = \frac{\Box}{12}$ 6 $\frac{1}{6} = \frac{\Box}{12}$ 7 $\frac{1}{2} = \frac{\Box}{6} = \frac{\Box}{12}$ 8 $\frac{1}{4} = \frac{\Box}{12}$

Write and complete the following.

9 $\frac{2}{3} = \frac{\Box}{6} = \frac{\Box}{12}$ 10 $\frac{3}{4} = \frac{\Box}{8} = \frac{\Box}{12}$ 11 $\frac{5}{6} = \frac{\Box}{12}$

F Write the following fractions putting in the missing numerator or denominator.

1 $\frac{3}{5} = \frac{n}{10}$ 2 $\frac{4}{5} = \frac{8}{d}$ 3 $\frac{3}{8} = \frac{n}{16}$ 4 $\frac{5}{8} = \frac{10}{d}$
5 $\frac{5}{12} = \frac{n}{24}$ 6 $\frac{3}{10} = \frac{6}{d}$ 7 $\frac{7}{10} = \frac{n}{100}$ 8 $\frac{9}{10} = \frac{90}{d}$
9 $\frac{2}{10} = \frac{n}{5}$ 10 $\frac{4}{10} = \frac{2}{d}$ 11 $\frac{10}{12} = \frac{n}{6}$ 12 $\frac{14}{16} = \frac{7}{d}$
13 $\frac{15}{20} = \frac{3}{d}$ 14 $\frac{10}{25} = \frac{n}{5}$ 15 $\frac{50}{100} = \frac{1}{d}$ 16 $\frac{75}{100} = \frac{n}{4}$

Change each of these fractions to hundredths.

17 $\frac{1}{5}$ 18 $\frac{2}{5}$ 19 $\frac{3}{5}$ 20 $\frac{4}{5}$
21 $\frac{1}{10}$ 22 $\frac{3}{10}$ 23 $\frac{7}{10}$ 24 $\frac{9}{10}$

G

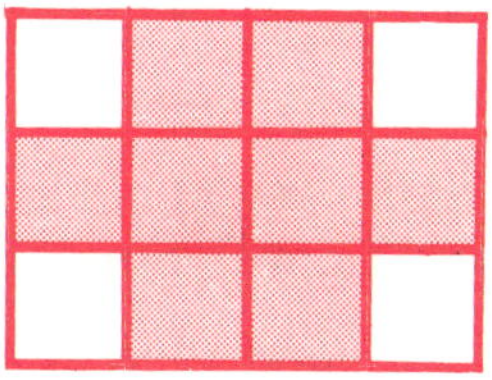

1 How many tiles are there in the drawing?
How many of them are
2 white   3 coloured?
How many twelfths (12ths) of the drawing are
4 white   5 coloured?
6 Write each of the fractions in its **lowest terms**.

Look at the drawings. Write in its lowest terms the fraction of each which is white; is coloured.

7  8 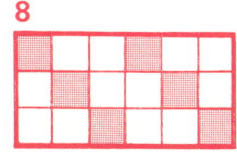 9

UNIT 10
Length mm cm

A In the drawing below, each point has been named by a letter.

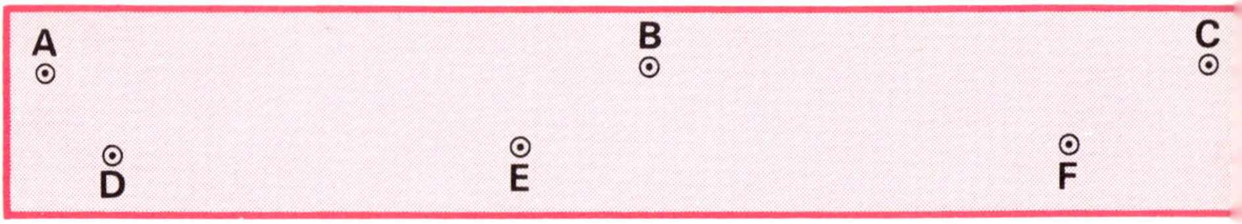

```
A              B                    C
⊙              ⊙                    ⊙

   ⊙              ⊙         ⊙
   D              E         F
```

Use a ruler marked in cm and ½ cm to find the measurement to the **nearest cm** between the points

1	A and B	2	A and E	3	B and D	4	A and
5	C and F	6	C and D	7	D and E	8	C and
9	F and B	10	E and C	11	F and D	12	C and

B Look at the ruler below, which is marked in cm and mm.
How many mm are there in

1	5 cm	2	7 cm	3	9 cm	4	10 cm
5	1 cm 8 mm	6	4 cm 9 mm	7	10 cm 5 mm	8	12 cm 6 mm

Change the following to cm and mm.

9	25 mm	10	42 mm	11	96 mm	12	108 mm
13	53 mm	14	99 mm	15	81 mm	16	74 mm

Look at the example.   54 mm = 5 cm 4 mm = 5.4 cm

Write first as cm and mm and then as cm.

17	38 mm	18	57 mm	19	92 mm	20	46 mm
21	125 mm	22	162 mm	23	184 mm	24	103 mm

Write as mm.

25	15 cm	26	8 cm 6 mm	27	3 cm 5 mm	28	9 cm 2 mm
29	6.9 cm	30	2.1 cm	31	10.3 cm	32	11.4 cm

C

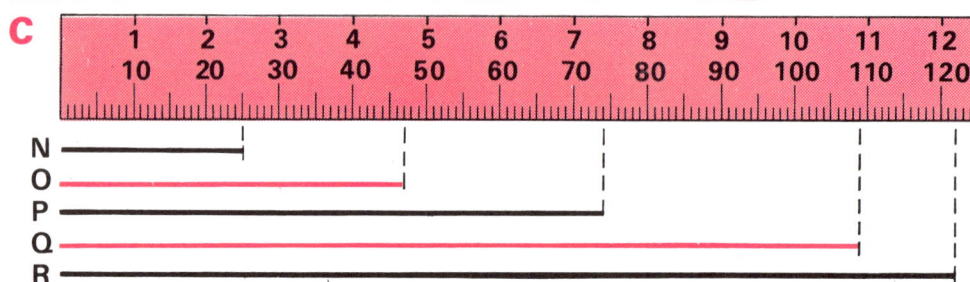

1 Write the length of each of the lines N, O, P, Q and R in mm; in cm and mm and then in cm. The first is done for you. 25 mm, 2 cm 5 mm, 2.5 cm

2 Measure and write the length of each line below in mm and then in cm.

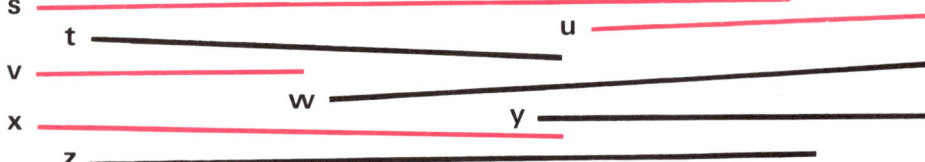

Check your answers before working the next section.

D Write to the nearest cm.
1 3.8 cm   2 4.4 cm   3 8.5 cm   4 30.1 cm
5 17.6 cm   6 10.2 cm   7 19.9 cm   8 6.3 cm
9 97 mm   10 88 mm   11 54 mm   12 167 mm
13 203 mm   14 706 mm   15 198 mm   16 302 mm

Look at your answers to **C1** and **C2**.
17 Write each measurement to the nearest cm.

E Measure and write the perimeter of each shape, first in mm and then in cm.

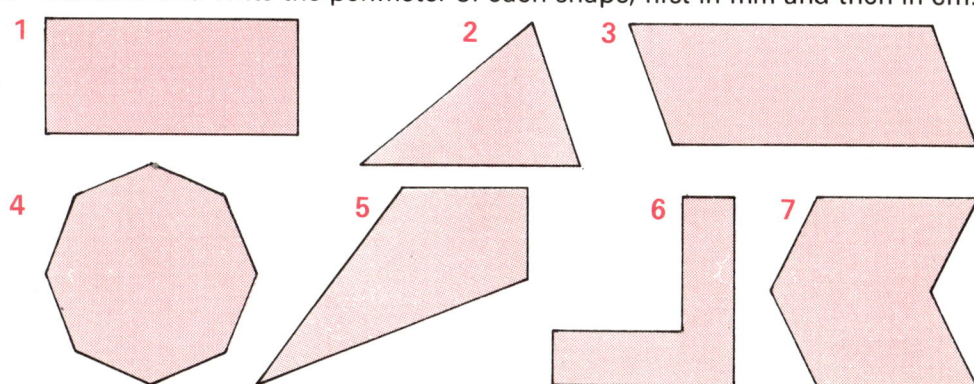

F Write each answer first in mm, then in cm.
1   6 mm   2   14 mm   3   20 mm   4   35 mm
     18 mm   19 mm   17 mm   10 mm
  + 16 mm   + 27 mm   + 33 mm   + 45 mm

5   13 mm   6   28 mm   7   25 mm   8   12 mm
     16 mm   27 mm   39 mm   26 mm
  + 14 mm   + 13 mm   + 18 mm   + 17 mm

Write each answer first in cm, then in mm.
9   3.4 cm   10   2.1 cm   11   3.2 cm   12   4.8 cm
     2.6 cm   4.4 cm   2.5 cm   2.2 cm
  + 4.0 cm   + 2.5 cm   + 1.3 cm   + 5.0 cm

13   2.8 cm   14   3.6 cm   15   2.9 cm   16   3.8 cm
     1.7 cm   1.4 cm   1.6 cm   2.5 cm
  + 4.9 cm   + 2.3 cm   + 4.2 cm   + 3.9 cm

G Write each answer first in mm, then in cm.
1   50 mm   2   110 mm   3   195 mm   4   258 mm
  − 30 mm   − 60 mm   − 95 mm   − 108 mm

5   193 mm   6   456 mm   7   550 mm   8   284 mm
  − 77 mm   − 129 mm   − 84 mm   − 87 mm

Write each answer first in cm, then in mm.
9   12.6 cm   10   18.0 cm   11   36.4 cm   12   23.9 cm
  − 3.6 cm   − 8.0 cm   − 18.4 cm   − 13.9 cm

13   4.2 cm   14   5.1 cm   15   12.5 cm   16   15.7 cm
  − 2.8 cm   − 2.6 cm   − 4.8 cm   − 3.9 cm

UNIT 11

Length   mm   cm   m   km

1 m = 100 cm

Half m or more—count to the **next** metre
Less than ½ m—count to the metre **below**

A Write to the nearest metre (m).
1 6 m 98 cm   2 15 m 48 cm   3 10 m 5 cm   4 19 m 50 cm
5 23 m 63 cm   6 11 m 16 cm   7 20 m 29 cm   8 14½ m

Write as m and cm.
9   321 cm   10 498 cm   11 935 cm   12 527 cm
13 711 cm   14 218 cm   15 705 cm   16 820 cm
17 905 cm   18 333 cm   19 690 cm   20 5½ m

Write as cm.
21 4 m   22 ¼ m   23 6 m 20 cm   24 8¾ m
25 5 m 19 cm   26 7 m 88 cm   27 3 m 37 cm   28 6 m 95 cm
29 2 m 50 cm   30 9 m 30 cm   31 2 m 8 cm   32 4 m 6 cm

2 m 46 cm = 2.46 m

B Write as m.
1 2 m 34 cm   2 4 m 27 cm   3 7 m 57 cm   4 3 m 19 cm
5 8 m 50 cm   6 1 m 5 cm   7 6 m 10 cm   8 5 m 7 cm
9 10 m 75 cm   10 12 m 20 cm   11 13 m 50 cm   12 10 m 5 cm

Write as cm.
13 2.38 m   14 5.62 m   15 4.26 m   16 3.75 m
17 9.84 m   18 6.83 m   19 7.50 m   20 8.10 m
21 1.06 m   22 2.09 m   23 12.42 m   24 10.27 m

C These plans of shapes are drawn to a scale of 1 cm to 1 metre.
1 Write. The scale is 1 cm to ☐ m or 1 cm to ☐ cm.

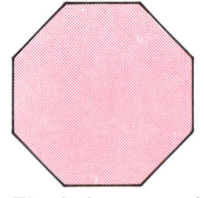

Find the actual measurement in m of the perimeter of
2 the rectangle   3 the acute-angled triangle   4 the octagon
5 the square   6 the right-angled triangle.

1 m = 1000 mm

D Write to the nearest m.
1 3 m 900 mm   2 4 m 300 mm   3 8 m 500 mm   4 8 m 250 mm
5 6 m 480 mm   6 7 m 825 mm   7 9 m 125 mm   8 5 m 634 mm

Write as m, or m and mm.
9   5000 mm   10 1600 mm   11 2200 mm   12 8750 mm
13 6498 mm   14 5716 mm   15 8509 mm   16 5205 mm
17 2028 mm   18 6090 mm   19 1005 mm   20 4006 mm

Write as mm.
21 6 m   22 7 m   23 6¼ m   24 2¾ m
25 7 m 125 mm   26 4 m 988 mm   27 2 m 750 mm   28 8 m 200 mm
29 9 m 20 mm   30 6 m 60 mm   31 1 m 5 mm   32 2 m 9 mm

E Write as m.   **1325 mm = 1.325 m**

1	4168 mm	2	3727 mm	3	8219 mm	4	7685 mm
5	6275 mm	6	4240 mm	7	1450 mm	8	9500 mm
9	5050 mm	10	2005 mm	11	1003 mm	12	950 mm

Write the answers first in mm, then in m.

13	852 mm 637 mm + 511 mm	14	1389 mm 976 mm + 1437 mm	15	3144 mm 2288 mm + 1499 mm	16	325 mm 160 mm + 415 mm
17	9730 mm − 1800 mm	18	4600 mm − 1900 mm	19	3270 mm − 1265 mm	20	5009 mm − 3208 mm
21	245 mm × 6	22	258 mm × 7	23	314 mm × 8	24	490 mm × 10
25	4)6752 mm	26	5)6850 mm	27	6)8400 mm	28	3)9312 mm

F Write to the nearest km.   **1 km = 1000 m**

1	5 km 300 m	2	$8\frac{1}{4}$ km	3	$9\frac{1}{2}$ km	4	$6\frac{3}{4}$ km
5	12 km 800 m	6	10 km 100 m	7	7 km 200 m	8	11 km 750 m
9	3 km 550 m	10	4 km 490 m	11	9 km 500 m	12	2 km 90 m

Write as km, or km and m.

13	4000 m	14	7000 m	15	2300 m	16	8900 m
17	5550 m	18	3890 m	19	1856 m	20	6125 m
21	3805 m	22	4109 m	23	2090 m	24	1080 m

Write as m.

25	6 km	26	3 km	27	5 km	28	10 km
29	7 km 700 m	30	4 km 200 m	31	$8\frac{1}{2}$ km	32	$6\frac{1}{4}$ km
33	$8\frac{3}{4}$ km	34	2 km 680 m	35	3 km 420 m	36	1 km 256 m

G The diagram shows the distance each child lives from school.

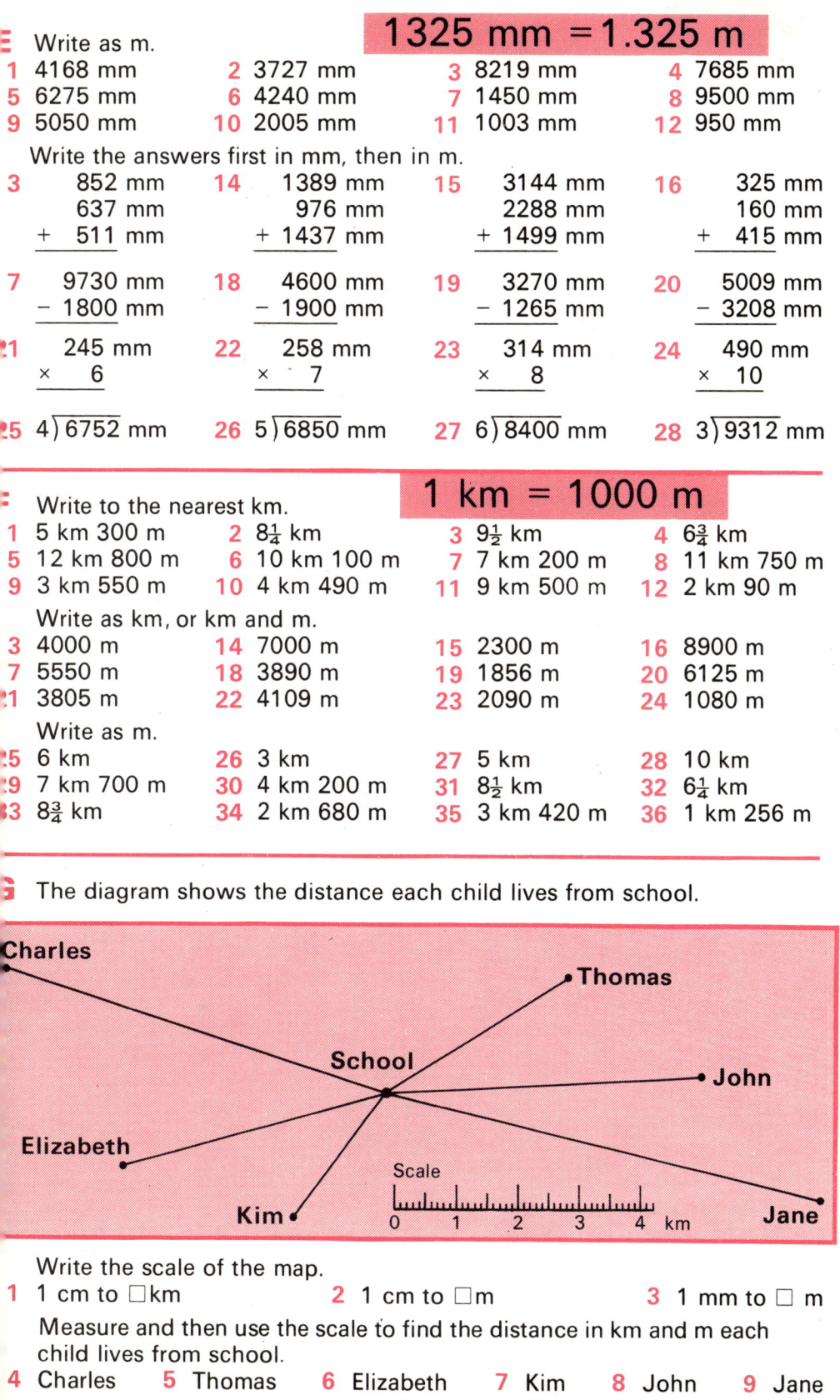

Write the scale of the map.

1 1 cm to ☐ km   2 1 cm to ☐ m   3 1 mm to ☐ m

Measure and then use the scale to find the distance in km and m each child lives from school.

4 Charles   5 Thomas   6 Elizabeth   7 Kim   8 John   9 Jane

25

UNIT 12
Looking back

A Turn back to **Unit 3** and work **Sections A** and **B** as quickly as possib[le]

B G 3564   H 5346   I 6435   J 4653

1 Write the value of the 3 in each of the numbers above.
 In the same way write the value of each **2** 4   **3** 5   **4** 6.
5 Write the length of each of the lines below to the **nearest 10 mm**.

```
mm 10  20  30  40  50  60  70  80  90  100
K ——
L ————————
M ——————————————————
N —————————————————————
O ———————————————————————————————————
```

Write each of the numbers below to the **nearest 10**.
6 69   **7** 54   **8** 95   **9** 112   **10** 167
11 283   **12** 318   **13** 222   **14** 655   **15** 996

Write each of the following to the **nearest 10p**.
16 £3·89   **17** £4·61   **18** £8·78   **19** £5·92   **20** £6·[ ]
21 £7·23   **22** £2·56   **23** £3·45   **24** £4·04   **25** £9·[ ]

C Look at the number line.

```
100  200  300  400  500  600  700  800  900  1[000]
       P    Q         R         S         T
```

1 Write the value of the numbers marked P, Q, R, S and T.
2 Now write each number P, Q, R, S and T to the **nearest 100**.
 Write each of these numbers to the **nearest 100**.
3 629   **4** 388   **5** 836   **6** 572   **7** 447
8 761   **9** 954   **10** 508   **11** 245   **12** 935

Write the following amounts to the **nearest £**.
13 £1·14 **14** £2·96 **15** £5·28 **16** £3·82 **17** £4·3[ ]
18 £6·73 **19** £7·67 **20** £14·51 **21** £28·49 **22** £39·[ ]

D 1 Write the members of each of these sets.
U = {multiples of 6 between 17 and 55}
V = {multiples of 7 between 20 and 64}
W = {multiples of 9 between 26 and 82}
X = {the factors of 12}   Y = {the factors of [ ]

2 Write the four prime numbers between 20 and 40.

Write the answers only.

Add ten to	**3** 9	**4** 99	**5** 999	**6** 999[ ]
Take ten from	**7** 100	**8** 1000	**9** 6009	**10** 10 0[ ]
Add one hundred to	**11** 54	**12** 308	**13** 1111	**14** 192[ ]
Take one hundred from	**15** 104	**16** 1111	**17** 7000	**18** 805[ ]
Add one thousand to	**19** 61	**20** 222	**21** 1111	**22** 906[ ]
Take one thousand from	**23** 1006	**24** 1111	**25** 10 081	**26** 15 3[ ]

26

E

Name the coins from those above which would be used to pay the following amounts. Use as few coins as possible.

| 1 | 54p | 2 | 18p | 3 | 63p | 4 | 27p | 5 | 45p | 6 | 90p |
| 7 | 36p | 8 | 72p | 9 | 81p | 10 | 99p | | | | |

F

Find the change from a FIFTY after spending

| 1 | 20p | 2 | 13p | 3 | 25p | 4 | 32p | 5 | 16p | 6 | 38p |
| 7 | 44p | 8 | 19p | 9 | 27p | 10 | 33p | 11 | 18p | 12 | 21p. |

Find the change from £1 after spending

| 13 | 70p | 14 | 57p | 15 | 24p | 16 | 35p | 17 | 62p | 18 | 11p |
| 19 | 88p | 20 | 16p | 21 | 43p | 22 | 25p | 23 | 59p | 24 | 34p. |

Find the change from £5 after spending

| 25 | 80p | 26 | 69p | 27 | 52p | 28 | 46p | 29 | 28p | 30 | £4·70 |
| 31 | £4·14 | 32 | £3·27 | 33 | £3·61 | 34 | £3·03 | 35 | £2·48 | 36 | £1·76. |

G

How many TWOS are worth

| 1 | 42p | 2 | 50p | 3 | 66p | 4 | 80p | 5 | £1·00? |

How many FIVES are worth

| 6 | 35p | 7 | 60p | 8 | 75p | 9 | 90p | 10 | £1·00 | 11 | £1·50 |
| 12 | £1·75 | 13 | £1·90 | 14 | £3·20 | 15 | £5·00? |

How many TENS are worth

| 16 | £1·40 | 17 | £1·90 | 18 | £2·50 | 19 | £3·00 | 20 | £3·70 | 21 | £4·10 |
| 22 | £5·00 | 23 | £6·40 | 24 | £8·30 | 25 | £10·00? |

H

How many TWENTIES are worth

| 1 | 80p | 2 | £1·00 | 3 | £1·80 | 4 | £2·20 | 5 | £2·60 | 6 | £3·40 |
| 7 | £4·40 | 8 | £5·00 | 9 | £8·00 | 10 | £10·00? |

How many FIFTIES are worth

| 11 | 150p | 12 | 400p | 13 | 500p | 14 | 700p | 15 | 1000p | 16 | £3·00 |
| 17 | £6·50 | 18 | £8·00 | 19 | £9·50 | 20 | £12? |

How many £s are worth

21	200p	22	600p	23	900p	24	1100p
25	1400p	26	40 TENS	27	70 TENS	28	10 TWENTIES
29	15 TWENTIES	30	20 TWENTIES?

I

Find the average of

1   9 cm, 8 cm, 6 cm, 5 cm   2   12 km, 18 km, 16 km, 17 km, 17 km
3   £12, £16, £18, £13, £24, £10   4   74p, 89p, 98p
5   35 kg, 40 kg, 27 kg, 59 kg, 44 kg, 36 kg, 32 kg.

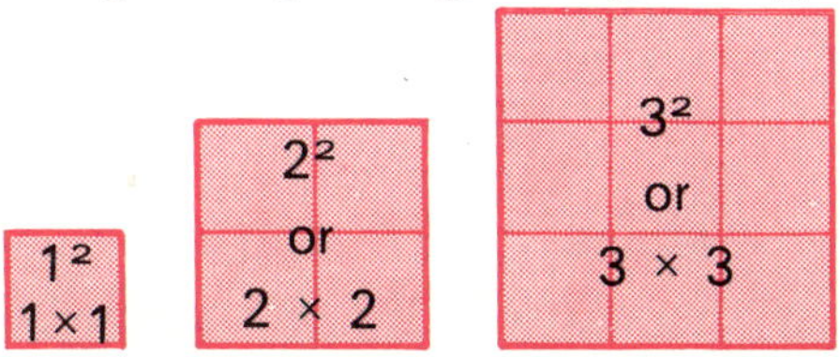

Write the value of

6   1^2 7 2^2 8 3^2.

Now write the value of

9   4^2 10 5^2 11 6^2 12 7^2
13   8^2 14 9^2 15 10^2

1^2
1×1

2^2
or
2×2

3^2
or
3×3

UNIT 13

Decimal fractions notation tenths

A Write the following numbers in figures.
1. four hundred
2. seven hundred and nine
3. five hundred and twenty
4. eight thousand
5. nine thousand and fifty-one
6. two thousand six hundred and fou[r]
7. seven thousand and seven
8. eight thousand and thirty

Write the value of each of the figures marked y and z in each of these numbers.

	y z		y z		y z		y
9	3044	10	8550	11	9972	12	562

	y z		y z		y z		y
13	2132	14	7170	15	1181	16	404

Write and complete.
17. 300 = ☐hundreds = ☐tens = ☐units
18. 810 = ☐hundreds ☐tens = ☐tens = ☐units
19. 1500 = ☐thousand ☐hundreds = ☐hundreds = ☐tens
20. 6400 = ☐thousands ☐hundreds = ☐hundreds = ☐tens

B

Multiply by 10
1. 4   2. 10   3. 30   4. 70   5. 90
6. 23   7. 56   8. 48   9. 11   10. 79
11. 100   12. 130   13. 270   14. 490   15. 580
16. 867   17. 531   18. 706   19. 367   20. 902

Multiply by 100
21. 5   22. 10   23. 20   24. 60   25. 70
26. 82   27. 39   28. 58   29. 71   30. 35

C

Divide by 10
1. 60   2. 90   3. 100   4. 300   5. 500
6. 340   7. 680   8. 710   9. 820   10. 940
11. 1000   12. 1560   13. 2480   14. 3270   15. 5030

Divide by 100
16. 900   17. 300   18. 1000   19. 2000   20. 8000
21. 4200   22. 1100   23. 3200   24. 10 000   25. 14 900

D Remember

To divide a number by 10, move the **digits one place to the right**.

T	U	tenths
1	5	
	1	5

$15 \div 10$
= 1 and 5 tenths = $1\frac{5}{10}$

Divide by 10
1. 12   2. 18   3. 23   4. 36   5. 58
6. 72   7. 89   8. 27   9. 63   10. 98
11. 123   12. 165   13. 239   14. 422   15. 187
16. 1687   17. 2354   18. 3095   19. 4608   20. 5005

Write and complete.
21. $1\frac{3}{10}$ = ☐tenths
22. $3\frac{7}{10}$ = ☐tenths
23. $2\frac{9}{10}$ = ☐tent[hs]
24. $4\frac{5}{10}$ = ☐tenths
25. $6\frac{6}{10}$ = ☐tenths
26. $5\frac{8}{10}$ = ☐tent[hs]

E

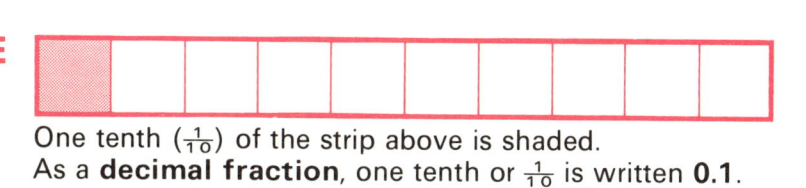

One tenth ($\frac{1}{10}$) of the strip above is shaded.
As a **decimal fraction**, one tenth or $\frac{1}{10}$ is written **0.1**.

1 Copy and complete this chart.

vulgar fractions	$\frac{1}{10}$	$\frac{2}{10}$	$\frac{3}{10}$	$\frac{4}{10}$	$\frac{5}{10}$	$\frac{6}{10}$
decimal fractions	0.1					

Each of these strips represents a **whole one**.

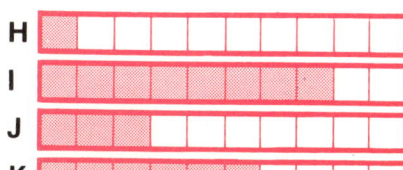

2 Write, first as a **vulgar fraction** and then as a **decimal fraction**, the part of each strip which is shaded.

3 In the same way, write each part which is unshaded.

4 For each strip, find the total of the shaded and unshaded parts.

Each shape below represents a whole one. Write as a **decimal fraction** the part of each which is 5 shaded 6 unshaded.

M 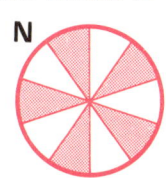 N 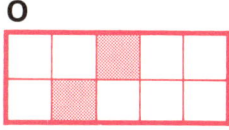 O P 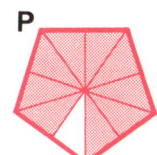 Q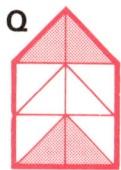

7 For each shape, find the total of the shaded and unshaded parts.

F This centimetre is divided into 10 millimetres.   1 cm

Write as a decimal fraction of a centimetre

1 1 mm   2 8 mm   3 6 mm   4 5 mm   5 3 mm.

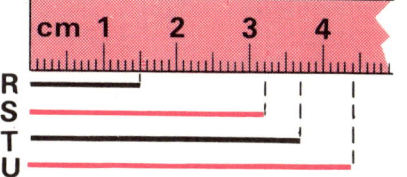

Write the length of each of the lines R, S, T and U
6 in mm
7 in cm and mm
8 in cm as a decimal.

9 Measure each line below and write its length in cm as a decimal.

V ———————————
W ———————
X ———
Y ——————————
Z ———————————————

G Write each of these numbers as a decimal.

	H	T	U	tenths
1			9	3
2		2	4	7
3	1	1	5	9

	H	T	U	tenths
4	2	0	3	4
5	1	6	0	8
6	2	0	0	6

Write each of the following as a decimal fraction.
7 27 tenths   8 86 tenths   9 51 tenths   10 109 tenths

29

UNIT 14
Mass grams kilograms

A

Which of the measures above, would you use to find a mass of
1. 1½ kg
2. ¼ kg
3. ¾ kg
4. 70 g
5. 700 g
6. 850 g
7. 1 kg 350 g
8. 1 kg 650 g

Write in tenths of 1 kg and then as a decimal fraction of 1 kg
9. 100 g
10. 300 g
11. 900 g
12. 700 g
13. 200 g
14. 600 g
15. 400 g
16. 800 g.

How many g less than 1 kg is
17. 200 g
18. 650 g
19. 380 g
20. 520 g
21. ¼ kg
22. 570 g
23. 0.2 kg
24. 0.9 kg?

How many g greater than ½ kg is
25. 800 g
26. 950 g
27. 620 g
28. 590 g
29. ¾ kg
30. 710 g
31. 0.6 kg
32. 0.9 kg?

B 1 Find the mass of each of the parcels X, Y and Z.

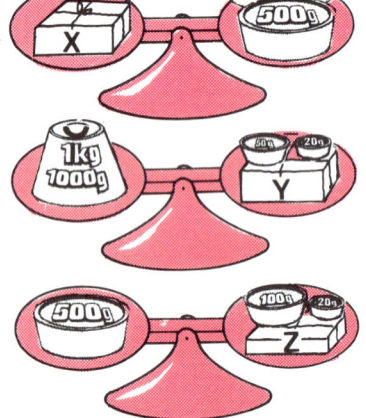

The diagram shows the dial on a weighing machine used for finding the mass of children. Find
2. the maximum mass that can be shown on the dial
3. the mass represented by one small division
4. the mass of each child shown by the pointers k, l, m and n
5. the total mass of the four children
6. their average mass.
7. What is your own mass in kg?
8. By how many kg is your mass greater or less than the average mass of the four children?

Find, from dials U, V and W
9. the maximum mass that can be shown on each
10. the mass represented by one small division on each.

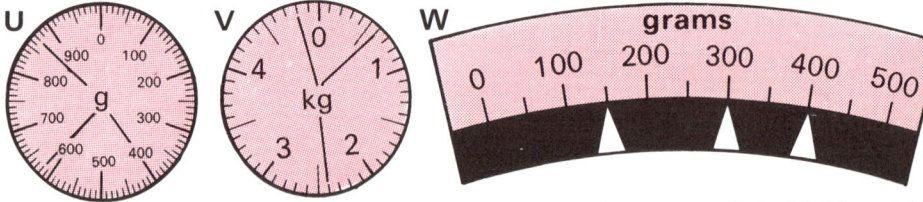

11. Read the mass shown by each of the three pointers on dials U, V and W

C Write to the nearest $\frac{1}{2}$ kg.
1. 2 kg 100 g
2. 1 kg 400 g
3. 3 kg 600 g
4. 4 kg 900 g
5. 1 kg 700 g
6. 3 kg 300 g
7. 4 kg 800 g
8. 2 kg 200 g
9. 6 kg 350 g
10. 5 kg 650 g
11. 8 kg 270 g
12. 7 kg 370 g

Write to the nearest kg.
13. 1 kg 80 g
14. 3 kg 900 g
15. 2 kg 250 g
16. 4 kg 750 g
17. 6 kg 350 g
18. 4 kg 630 g
19. 8.3 kg
20. 5.5 kg

D Write as kg and g.
1. 7000 g
2. 1500 g
3. 3600 g
4. 2550 g
5. 1460 g
6. 3870 g
7. 4910 g
8. 6120 g
9. 8540 g
10. 7090 g
11. 5080 g
12. 4008 g

Write as g.
13. 8 kg
14. $5\frac{1}{2}$ kg
15. $3\frac{1}{4}$ kg
16. 1 kg 700 g
17. 3 kg 400 g
18. 6 kg 150 g
19. 4 kg 360 g
20. 3 kg 50 g
21. 5 kg 70 g
22. 1 kg 10 g
23. 10 kg 500 g
24. 20 kg 300 g

1230 g = 1.230 kg

E Write as kg.
1. 3350 g
2. 2160 g
3. 1730 g
4. 2980 g
5. 6100 g
6. 3200 g
7. 2010 g
8. 4040 g
9. 3070 g
10. 600 g
11. 750 g
12. 20 g

Find the missing mass in each of the following.
Write each mass, first as g and then as kg.
13. 570 g + ☐ g = 1 kg
14. 130 g + ☐ g = 0.5 kg
15. 1 kg − ☐ g = 460 g
16. $\frac{1}{2}$ kg − ☐ g = 80 g
17. 2 kg − 1750 g = ☐ g
18. 800 g + ☐ g = 1.5 kg
19. 250 g + ☐ g = 0.4 kg
20. 0.7 kg − ☐ g = 200 g

F
1. 800 g + 350 g + 80 g + 160 g = ☐ kg ☐ g = ☐ kg
2. Find the difference in g between 2.5 kg and 1750 g.
3. The total mass of 3 parcels is 2 kg 700 g. Find the average mass.
4. How many g must be added to 1 kg 800 g to make $2\frac{3}{4}$ kg?

   A tin of soup has a mass of 300 g. Find the mass in kg of
5. 5 tins
6. 9 tins.
7. A box has a mass of 370 g and another box is three times as heavy. Find the total mass in kg of the two boxes.
8. The total mass of 10 apples is 1.5 kg. Find the average mass, in g, of one apple.
9. How many 300 g packets of tea can be made from 4.5 kg?
10. 7 × 250 g. Give the answer in kg.
11. Share 2.1 kg of sweets equally among 7 children. How many g will each child receive?

31

UNIT 15

Capacity millilitres (ml) litres

A | 1 litre = 1000 millilitres (ml) |

How many ml are there in
1. ½ litre
2. ¼ litre
3. 1/10 litre?
4. Write and complete. 1/10 litre = 0.1 litre = ☐ ml

Find the missing number of ml.
5. 0.5 litre = ☐ ml
6. 0.3 litre = ☐ ml
7. 0.7 litre = ☐ ml
8. 0.2 litre = ☐ ml
9. 0.6 litre = ☐ ml
10. 0.9 litre = ☐ ml

How many ml less than 1 litre is
11. 400 ml
12. 850 ml
13. 640 ml
14. 0.5 litre
15. 0.8 litre?

How many ml greater than ½ litre is
16. 650 ml
17. 770 ml
18. 595 ml
19. 0.9 litre
20. 0.6 litre?

A medicine spoon measures 5 ml.
How many spoonfuls of medicine are there in bottles holding
21. 500 ml
22. 300 ml
23. 200 ml
24. 150 ml
25. 50 ml?

B Change to litres, or litres and ml.
1. 3000 ml
2. 8000 ml
3. 2500 ml
4. 1200 ml
5. 3450 ml
6. 1050 ml
7. 6080 ml
8. 5030 ml

Write and complete.
9. 1250 ml = ☐ litre ☐ ml = ☐ litres
10. 4060 ml = ☐ litres ☐ ml = ☐ litres
11. 2700 ml = ☐ litres ☐ ml = ☐ litres
12. 5010 ml = ☐ litres ☐ ml = ☐ litres

Write as litres.
13. 2020 ml
14. 3500 ml
15. 1050 ml
16. 800 ml
17. 6200 ml
18. 250 ml
19. 4070 ml
20. 90 ml

Change to ml.
21. 3 litres 300 ml
22. 2 litres 650 ml
23. 5 litres 50 ml
24. 4¼ litres
25. 3¾ litres
26. 1.5 litres

C Write to the nearest litre.
1. 6 litres 300 ml
2. 4 litres 450 ml
3. 9 litres 850 ml
4. 7 litres 720 ml
5. 3 litres 60 ml
6. 2 litres 680 ml

Write to the nearest ½ litre (0.5 litre).
7. 2 litres 300 ml
8. 5 litres 150 ml
9. 8 litres 700 ml
10. 9 litres 850 ml
11. 10 litres 300 ml
12. 14.6 litres

Find the missing measure in each of the following.
Write each answer first as ml, then as litres.
13. 230 ml + ☐ ml = 1 litre
14. 370 ml + ☐ ml = 0.5 litre
15. 1 litre − ☐ ml = 340 ml
16. ½ litre − ☐ ml = 410 ml
17. 450 ml + ☐ ml = 1½ litres
18. 3 litres − ☐ ml = 2150 ml
19. 130 ml + ☐ ml = 0.4 litre
20. 0.6 litre − ☐ ml = 50 ml

The amount of water each
container holds when full is
given in litres or millilitres,
which are measures of capacity.
Which of the containers
A, B, C or D hold
1 more than 1 litre
2 less than 1 litre?
Which of the containers has
3 the greatest capacity
4 the least capacity?
5 Find their difference in mℓ.

By how many mℓ is the capacity of
6 A greater than that of B   7 B less than that of C?
Find the capacity of a container which is
8 half that of A   9 three times that of D.
10 A bucket has the same capacity as the four containers together.
Find the amount of water the bucket holds in litres.
Which two of the containers together have a capacity of
11 1750 mℓ   12 2750 mℓ?

The picture shows a glass cylinder which can be used for
measuring, in mℓ, small amounts of liquid.
1 What is the greatest amount of liquid which can be
measured in the cylinder?
2 Read from the scale the number of mℓ which are
represented by each division.
3 Find the amount of liquid, to the nearest 10 mℓ, shown by
the arrows marked R, S, T and U.

The drawings X and Y show
the water level in two more
measuring cylinders, the scales
of which are marked in mℓ.
4 Read in mℓ the amount of water in
the cylinder as shown on X; on Y.
5 By how many mℓ is each of the
amounts less than 100 mℓ?
6 How much more water is shown
on Y than on X?

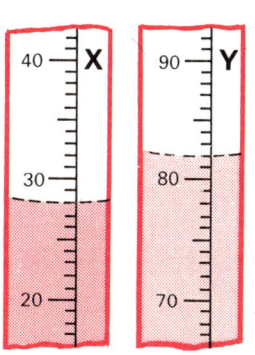
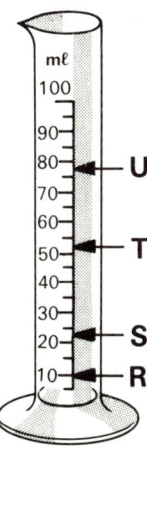

1 Find the total of 1½ litres, 950 mℓ and 2.4 litres.
2 By how many mℓ is 1.8 litres less than 3½ litres?
3 A dish holds 780 mℓ. Find in litres how much 5 such dishes hold.
4 How many glasses each holding 150 mℓ can be filled from 1.5 litres of
orange squash?
5 Which is the greater and by how many mℓ
¼ of 3 litres 360 mℓ   or   ⅕ of 4.3 litres?

33

UNIT 16

Number, money, measures
addition and subtraction

A Write the answers only when you can.
1. (5 + 5) + 7
2. 35 + 5 + 7
3. 55 + 5 +
4. (7 + 3) + 8
5. 27 + 3 + 8
6. 33 + 7 +
7. (8 + 2) + 6
8. 48 + 2 + 6
9. 72 + 8 +
10. (9 + 1) + 5
11. 59 + 1 + 5
12. 91 + 9 +
13. (6 + 4) + 9
14. 76 + 4 + 9
15. 84 + 6 +
16. 37 + 43
17. 28 + 52
18. 69 + 21
19. 76 + 24
20. 60 + 49
21. 80 + 38
22. 67 + 70
23. 94 + 70
24. 37 + 56
25. 49 + 35
26. 73 + 18
27. 69 + 24
28. 26 + 85
29. 94 + 48
30. 68 + 35
31. 83 + 89
32. 140 + 30
33. 120 + 60
34. 170 + 30
35. 250 + 5
36. 190 + 80
37. 280 + 150
38. 490 + 190
39. 370 + 1
40. 260 + 290
41. 670 + 270
42. 560 + 380
43. 490 + 4

B Write the answers only.

1. 9.4 cm
   5.3 cm
   + 7.8 cm

2. 2.6 km
   5.0 km
   + 8.4 km

3. 7.2 cm
   9.3 cm
   + 6.6 cm

4. 5.1 km
   8.9 km
   + 7.4 km

5. £
   4·68
   2·30
   1·95
   + 6·71

6. £
   1·53
   0·68
   8·27
   + 3·49

7. £
   9·04
   3·19
   8·56
   + 1·78

8. £
   3·76
   0·75
   1·94
   + 8·93

9. kg
   6.200
   2.030
   1.450
   + 9.640

10. litres
    9.320
    4.260
    7.670
    + 3.090

11. kg
    1.290
    7.860
    2.580
    + 4.740

12. litres
    8.630
    3.040
    7.580
    + 1.750

13. 238 + 16 + 987 + 3040 + 65
14. 104 + 8 + 67 + 1367 + 9
15. 75 + 236 + 89 + 947 + 18

C
1.
7	8	3
	10	
	4	5

2.
18	15	
	20	
	25	22

3.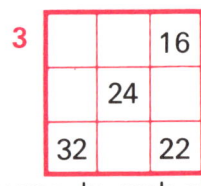

4.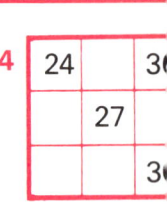

Draw and complete these number squares. In each of the squares, each row, column and diagonal must add up to the same total.

Look at the numbers below.

| 18 | 23 | 27 | 29 | 36 | 41 | 54 | 60 |

Find the total of
5. the odd numbers
6. the even numbers
7. the prime numbe
8. Find the sum of all the multiples of 2 between 93 and 109.

D Write the answers only when you can.
1. 10 − 7
2. 20 − 7
3. 40 − 7
4. 80 − 7
5. 13 − 6
6. 23 − 6
7. 73 − 6
8. 93 − 6
9. 28 − 19
10. 48 − 19
11. 68 − 19
12. 88 − 19
13. 46 − 17
14. 56 − 17
15. 76 − 17
16. 96 − 17
17. 31 − 18
18. 51 − 18
19. 71 − 18
20. 91 − 18
21. 110 − 50
22. 140 − 70
23. 120 − 90
24. 130 − 60
25. 260 − 80
26. 370 − 90
27. 450 − 160
28. 520 − 170
29. 135 − 72
30. 128 − 49
31. 163 − 85
32. 176 − 98
33. 218 − 99
34. 217 − 48
35. 131 − 45
36. 122 − 66

Find the difference between
37. 56 and 28
38. 82 and 37
39. 41 and 23
40. 29 and 71
41. 65 and 92
42. 18 and 81
43. 75 and 56
44. 45 and 29.

E
1. 3.8 cm − 1.9 cm
2. 15.6 km − 4.7 km
3. 23.0 cm − 14.6 cm
4. 14.5 km − 3.9 km
5. £4·07 − £2·88
6. £15·19 − £1·70
7. £23·00 − £5·35
8. £9·27 − £1·29
9. 15.00 m − 4.25 m
10. 18.50 m − 1.75 m
11. 3.20 m − 1.80 m
12. 6.10 m − 1.65 m
13. 1.250 litres − 0.600 litres
14. 1.750 litres − 0.900 litres
15. 3.500 litres − 1.250 litres
16. 6.280 litres − 2.750 litres
17. 8.000 kg − 1.750 kg
18. 5.150 kg − 1.700 kg
19. 10.500 kg − 1.360 kg
20. 7.400 kg − 2.250 kg

F
1. Find the value of each letter.
$29 + a = 111$
$137 + b = 190$
$c + 42 = 201$
$d + 94 = 500$
$256 + e = 1000$
$4.8 + f = 10$
6.3 cm $+ x$ cm $= 9$ cm
$£y + £1·47 = £2·72$
z km $+ 8.5$ km $= 12$ km

Find each missing amount.
2. £5·27 − £□·□□ = £2·38
3. £3·31 − £□·□□ = £1·80
4. £10·00 − £□·□□ = £4·17
5. £5·50 − £□·□□ = £2·26
6. £1·14 + £1·18 + £□·□□ = £5·00
7. £2·38 + £□·□□ + £1·23 = £6·74
8. £□·□□ + £1·66 + £3·54 = £8·13
9. £6·32 + £1·29 + £□·□□ = £9·40

Subtract
10. 437 from 811
11. 962 from 3000
12. 743 from 2222
13. 180 from 2010
14. 508 from 1213
15. 394 from 1200.

UNIT 17

Time   24-hour clock   The calendar

A Copy and complete the charts.

1.
12-hour clock times	2.00a.m.	4.00a.m.	6.00a.m.	8.00a.m.	10.00a.m.	12.00 noon
24-hour clock times	02.00					

2.
24-hour clock times	13.00	15.00	17.00	19.00	21.00	23.00
12-hour clock times						

Change these **a.m. times** to 24-hour clock times.

- **3** 1.10
- **4** 11.50
- **5** 4.20
- **6** 10.40
- **7** half past 8
- **8** quarter to 6
- **9** quarter past 3
- **10** 5 past 5
- **11** 5.08
- **12** 3.17
- **13** 11.56
- **14** 6.33
- **15** 11 min past 11
- **16** 8 min to 7
- **17** 3 min past 2
- **18** 27 min to 9

B Change these **p.m. times** to 24-hour clock times.

- **1** 7.10
- **2** 3.20
- **3** 5.50
- **4** 11.40
- **5** 10.25
- **6** 4.35
- **7** 2.05
- **8** 6.55
- **9** half past 2
- **10** quarter to 8
- **11** quarter past 4
- **12** 20 to 12
- **13** 7.07
- **14** 9.18
- **15** 5.47
- **16** 8.03
- **17** 18 min past 1
- **18** 26 min to 5
- **19** 28 min past 3
- **20** 6 min past 12

Change these **24-hour clock times** to a.m. or p.m.

- **21** 03.19
- **22** 13.47
- **23** 14.16
- **24** 21.12
- **25** 11.27
- **26** 17.3
- **27** 01.10
- **28** 22.09
- **29** 18.54
- **30** 08.10
- **31** 12.45
- **32** 00.0

C How many minutes in

- **1** 1 h 20 min
- **2** 1 h 50 min
- **3** $2\frac{1}{4}$ hours
- **4** $2\frac{1}{2}$ hours
- **5** $3\frac{1}{2}$ hours
- **6** $1\frac{3}{4}$ hours
- **7** 5 hours
- **8** 3 h 55 min

Change to h and min.

- **9** 70 min
- **10** 100 min
- **11** 180 min
- **12** 170 min
- **13** 240 min
- **14** 160 min
- **15** 215 min
- **16** 600 min

D How many min, or h and min is it from

- **1** 8.45 a.m. to 11 a.m.
- **2** 9.50 a.m. to 10.20 a.m.
- **3** 6.40 a.m. to 7.30 a.m.
- **4** 3.20 p.m. to 5.40 p.m.
- **5** 10.07 p.m. to 11.52 p.m.
- **6** 9.24 p.m. to 10.19 p.m.
- **7** 8.17 a.m. to noon
- **8** 11.35 a.m. to 1.00 p.m.
- **9** 10.50 a.m. to 1.30 p.m.
- **10** 9.45 a.m. to 2.15 p.m.
- **11** 10.23 a.m. to 1.40 p.m.
- **12** 8.15 a.m. to 1.50 p.m.?

E

London	East Croydon	Lewes	Eastbourne	Bexhill	Hastings
11.48	12.04	12.49	13.11	13.32	13.42

1 Write each of the times shown on the timetable as 12-hour clock times.

From the timetable, find the time taken from London to

- **2** East Croydon
- **3** Lewes
- **4** Eastbourne
- **5** Bexhill
- **6** Hastings
- **7** Lewes to Bexhill
- **8** East Croydon to Eastbourne.

F

1 How many months are there in a year?

Name the months in which there are
2 30 days 3 31 days.
4 How many days are there in a year when there are 29 days in February?
5 What is the special name given to this year?
6 Which of these years were Leap Years?
1604   1890   1928   1957   1967   1972   1980

| July | Aug. | Jan. | Feb. | Oct. | Nov. | April | May |

Which of the months named above fall in each of the seasons
7 spring   8 autumn   9 summer   10 winter?

Write both the **day** and the **date** of each child's return from holiday.

		on holiday from	return from holiday
1	Tim	Fri. 14th May	the following Thursday
2	Mary	Wed. 28th July	after two weeks
3	John	Sun. 27th June	after ten days
4	Sally	Tues. 17th Aug.	21st September
5	Philip	Sat. 25th Sept.	after four weeks

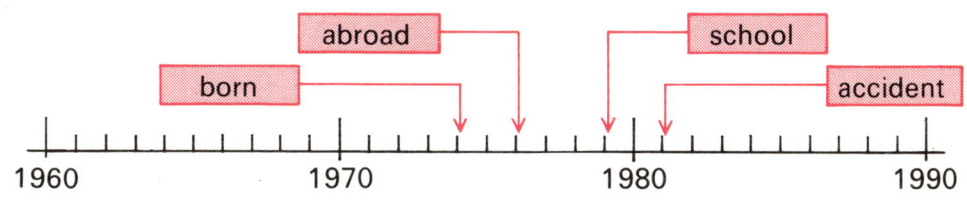

G

David made this time-line to show some important dates in his life.
Write the year in which
1 he was born   2 he had an accident   3 he started school
4 he went abroad.

How old was David when
5 he went abroad   6 he started school   7 he had an accident?
8 Give David's age in 1990.

In which year was each of the following born?
9 Mary who is 9 years older than David.
10 Debbie who is 4 years younger than David.
11 David's uncle who will be 36 in 1999.

H

The chart shows the birth dates of five children.

Thomas	31.10.80
Claire	30.11.74
Martin	30. 4.76
Mary	29. 2.73
Joan	28. 8.77

1 Write the names of the children in order, the oldest first.
2 Find the age in years and months of each child on 1st December 1990.
Counting to the nearest month, how many years and months older is
3 Mary than Joan   4 Martin than Thomas
5 Joan than Thomas   6 Claire than Joan?

37

UNIT 18
Lines and angles

A Each line in this shape has been named by using two capital letters.

Name the line or lines which are
1. vertical
2. horizontal
3. oblique
4. parallel to the base AB
5. perpendicular to the base.

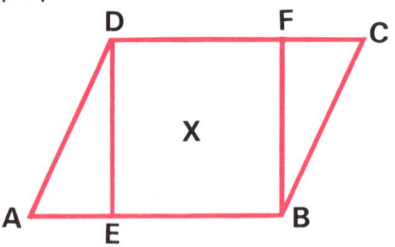

6. Name the line in shape X which is the base.

Which lines in shape X are
7. perpendicular to the base
8. perpendicular to DC?

Name the line which is parallel to
9. AB
10. AD
11. DE

B An angle is named by using three capital letters

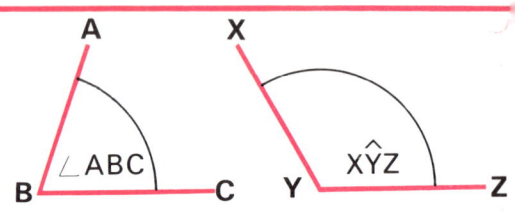

The symbols ∠ or ^ are short ways of writing **angle**.

Use a set square. Find and name the angles below which are
1. acute angles
2. obtuse angles
3. right angles.

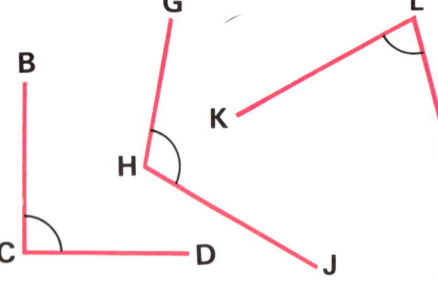

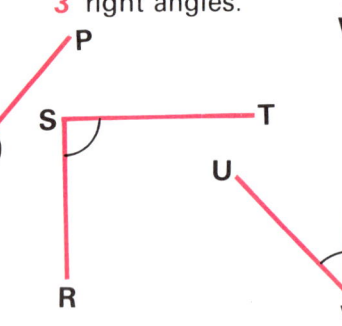

Use set squares to draw the following angles.
4. ∠ABC = 90°
5. ∠DEF = 45°
6. HÔK = 60°
7. STÛ = 30°
8. a straight angle BOC
9. ∠CDE = 120°
10. TÔP = 150°
11. ∠MNO = 135°

> **Remember** Angles measure turns or rotations.
> 1 complete turn = 4 right angles = 360°.

12. How many right angles are there in the marked angles at the centre of each of these circles?

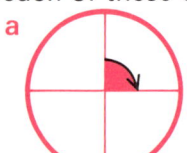

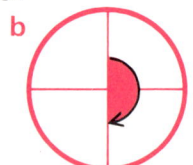

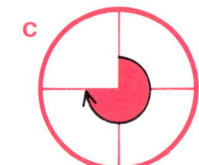

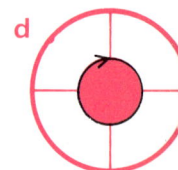

a   b   c   d

13. How many degrees are there in each marked angle?

C Robert stands facing North.

Through how many right angles does he turn **clockwise** to face

1 East   **2** West   **3** South

anti-clockwise to face

4 West   **5** East   **6** South?

Through how many right angles does he turn **clockwise** from

7 East to West   **8** South to East

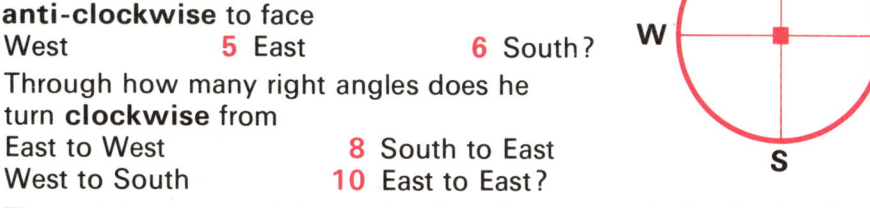

9 West to South   **10** East to East?

Through how many right angles does he turn **anti-clockwise** from

11 South to East   **12** East to West   **13** South to West   **14** East to East?

How many degrees are there in

15 ½ right angle   **16** a straight angle?

In each circle below, the angles shown at the centre are equal.

17 Find, in degrees, the size of each marked angle.

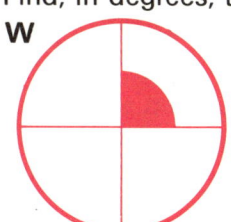

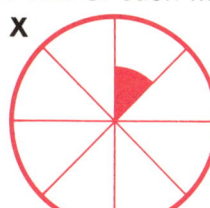

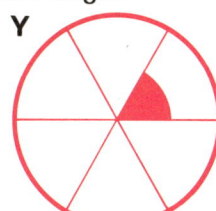

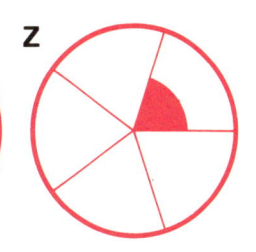

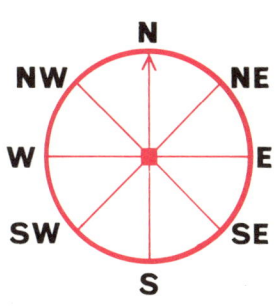

W   X   Y   Z

D Susan is facing North.

Through how many degrees does she turn **clockwise** to face

1 NE   **2** SE   **3** SW   **4** NW?

Through how many degrees does she turn **clockwise** from

5 SE to S   **6** SW to N   **7** E to SW

8 NW to SW   **9** W to SE   **10** NE to W

11 S to SE   **12** SW to E   **13** SE to NE?

E The map shows the positions of five scouts.

In which direction will each of these scouts have to walk to reach the camp?

1 Alan   **2** David

3 Ian   **4** Tim

5 Peter

6 Use a ruler and the given scale to find the distance to the nearest kilometre each scout has to walk.

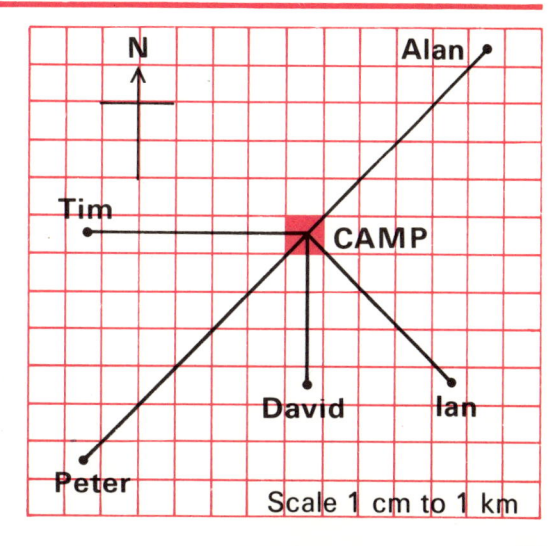

Scale 1 cm to 1 km

39

UNIT 19
Looking back

A Turn back to **Unit 6** and work **A**4, 5, 6; **B**4, 5, 6 and **C**4, 5, 6 as quickly as possible.

B These odometers show the distances travelled by four cars.
Th H T U t

0 0 8 6 8 4	0 1 0 0 9 8	0 9 6 3 4 5	0 1 9 9 9 6
Car W	Car X	Car Y	Car Z

1 Write as a decimal the number of km travelled by each car.
How much further will each car have travelled when the readings are as follows:

Car W	Car X	Car Y	Car Z
2 0 0 8 7 0 0	5 0 1 0 1 0 0	8 0 9 7 0 0 0	11 0 5 0 0 0 0
3 0 1 0 0 0 0	6 0 1 1 1 1 0	9 1 0 0 0 0 0	12 0 9 2 3 6 0
4 0 1 9 4 7 2	7 0 2 0 0 0 0	10 1 0 7 8 2 4	13 1 0 3 7 5 5

Write in figures.
14 2 hundred point 1
15 4 thousand 3 hundred and 9 point 2
16 3 thousand and 6 point 7
17 1 thousand 1 hundred point 3
18 8 thousand and 10 point 6
19 5 thousand 2 hundred and 20 point 9

C Write the length of each of the lines below
1 in mm 2 in cm 3 to the nearest cm.

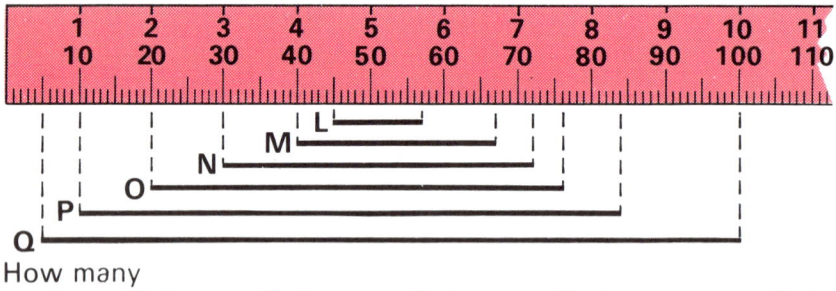

How many
cm in   4 3 m   5 5 m   6 $\frac{1}{2}$ m   7 $\frac{1}{4}$ m   8 $\frac{3}{4}$ m
mm in   9 5 cm   10 8$\frac{1}{2}$ cm   11 10 cm   12 50 cm   13 1 m
g in   14 $\frac{1}{2}$ kg   15 $\frac{1}{4}$ kg   16 $\frac{3}{4}$ kg   17 1.360 kg   18 2.500 kg
ml in   19 $\frac{1}{2}$ litre   20 $\frac{1}{4}$ litre   21 $\frac{3}{4}$ litre   22 2.450 litres   23 3.050 litres

D Write these measures in order of size, the largest first.
1 6.9 cm   408 mm   3 m   1.57 m   1.235 m
2 3 kg   2050 g   2$\frac{1}{2}$ kg   2.180 kg   1.950 kg
3 2$\frac{1}{2}$ litres   3060 ml   2 litres   1.850 litres   3.100 litres

Write the answers in cm.
4 1 m − 27 cm   5 2 m − 1 m 36 cm   6 5 m − 3 m 25 cm
7 2 m 20 cm − 1 m 50 cm   8 5 m 37 cm − 1 m 40 cm
9 3.69 m − 1.44 m   10 4.28 m − 3.79 m   11 7.10 m − 5.63 m

Write the answers in g.
12 □ g + 575 g = 1 kg   13 $\frac{1}{2}$ kg − 250 g = □ g
14 2$\frac{1}{2}$ kg + □ g = 5 kg   15 1 kg − □ g = 370 g
16 □ g + 1 kg 60 g = 3 kg   17 5$\frac{1}{4}$ kg − 380 g = □ g

E   The picture shows a spring balance.
    What is the mass in kg and g shown by the pointers
1   W   2   X   3   Y   4   Z?
    Find
5   the total of the four masses
6   the average of the four masses.
7   By how many g is the lightest mass less than the average?
8   By how many g is the heaviest mass more than the average?
    What mass in kg and g is
9   three times that of X   10   half that of Y?

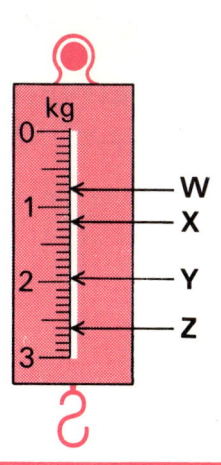

Write each answer as £s.
1   10 × 8p   2   10 × 48p   3   15p × 10   4   35p × 10
5   10 × £0·01   6   10 × £0·10   7   10 × £0·08   8   10 × £0·80
9   £0·16 × 10   10 £1·60 × 10   11 £0·24 × 10   12 £2·40 × 10
13 90p ÷ 10   14 70p ÷ 10   15 80p ÷ 10   16 £1·00 ÷ 10
17 £1·50 ÷ 10   18 £7·40 ÷ 10   19 £8·20 ÷ 10   20 £2·30 ÷ 10
21 £28·80 ÷ 10   22 £37·60 ÷ 10   23 £2·20 ÷ 10   24 £1·40 ÷ 10

The plan shows the distance and direction of five children's homes from school.
1   Write the scale of the plan.
    1 cm to ☐m or 1 mm to ☐m.
    Find the distance each child lives from school
2   in m   3   in km.
    Write the direction each child takes when
4   walking from home to school
5   returning home from school.
    Look at the compass rose on the plan.
    How many degrees are turned in a clockwise direction from
6   N to E   7   E to SE   8   W to NE   9   NW to NE
10 S to NW   11 SW to W   12 NE to S   13 SE to SW?
    Which of the angles in the answers to 6–13 are
14 acute angles   15 obtuse angles   16 right angles?

Find the value of the missing number in each example.

time	speed	distance
2 h	40 km/h	☐km
6 h	55 km/h	☐km
3 h	☐km/h	210 km

time	speed	distance
7 h	☐km/h	525 km
☐h	50 km/h	200 km
☐h	80 km/h	400 km

41

UNIT 20
Decimal fractions
notation tenths hundredths

A Write the number shown on each abacus picture as a decimal fraction.

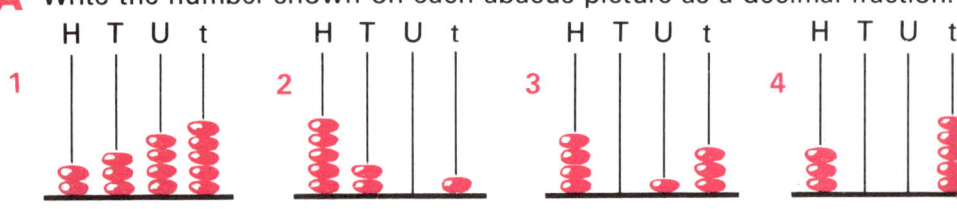

1 H T U t   2 H T U t   3 H T U t   4 H T U t

Draw abacus pictures to show these numbers.

5 $238\frac{6}{10}$ 6 $457\frac{3}{10}$ 7 301.9   8 680

Write and complete.

9 6.2 = ☐units ☐tenths = ☐tenths
10 4.3 = ☐units ☐tenths = ☐tenths
11 8.7 = ☐tenths   12 9.1 = ☐tenths   13 5.8 = ☐tenths
14 22.5 = ☐tenths   15 37.6 = ☐tenths   16 44.4 = ☐tenths

Write as decimals.

17 13 tenths   18 29 tenths   19 61 tenths   20 48 tenths
21 24 tenths   22 77 tenths   23 126 tenths   24 205 tenths

B Write the value of the figure underlined in each number.
1 3<u>7</u>9   2 7<u>3</u>.9   3 97<u>3</u>   4 79
5 52<u>6</u>.0   6 20<u>6</u>5   7 502.<u>6</u>   8 26

Make each of the following numbers 10 times bigger.
9 0.1   10 0.6   11 0.9   12 1.5   13 3.
14 5.3   15 9.4   16 12.8   17 30.9   18 50

Make each of these numbers 10 times smaller.
19 6   20 8   21 3   22 14   23 39
24 50   25 70   26 122   27 205   28 40

C X

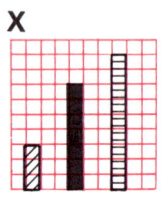

The large square X represents a whole one or one unit.
It has been divided into 100 small squares.
One small square is $\frac{1}{100}$ or **0.01** of the whole one.

Write first as a **vulgar fraction** and then as a **decimal fraction** the part of the whole one which is

1 shaded ▨   2 shaded ▬   3 shaded ☰

Write as a decimal fraction.

4 $\frac{2}{100}$ 5 $\frac{4}{100}$ 6 $\frac{5}{100}$ 7 $\frac{6}{100}$ 8 $\frac{}{1}$

Y

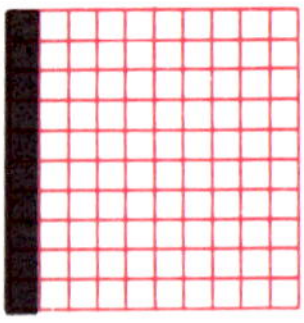

$\frac{1}{10}$ or 0.1 of the whole square Y is shaded.

9 Write and complete. $\frac{1}{10} = \frac{☐}{100}$

How many hundredths are there in

10 $\frac{2}{10}$ 11 $\frac{5}{10}$ 12 $\frac{7}{10}$ 13 $\frac{9}{10}$ 14 $\frac{6}{10}$
15 0.1   16 0.8   17 0.4   18 0.3   19 1.

Write the answers to the following as decimal fractions.

20 $\frac{7}{10} + \frac{3}{100}$ 21 $\frac{4}{10} + \frac{9}{100}$ 22 $\frac{1}{10} + \frac{7}{100}$ 23 $\frac{5}{10} + \frac{}{1}$
24 $\frac{8}{10} + \frac{1}{100}$ 25 $\frac{2}{10} + \frac{2}{100}$ 26 $\frac{9}{10} + \frac{5}{100}$ 27 $\frac{6}{10} + \frac{}{1}$

D Each large square represents one whole one.
Write as a **vulgar fraction** (in hundredths) the part of each whole one which is
1 shaded   2 unshaded.

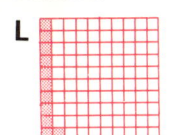

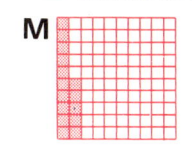

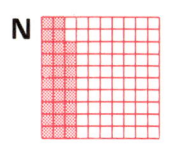

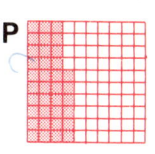

L   M   N   O   P

Now write as a **decimal fraction** the part of each whole one which is
3 shaded   4 unshaded.

Write as decimal fractions.

5 $\frac{28}{100}$ 6 $\frac{54}{100}$ 7 $\frac{72}{100}$ 8 $\frac{46}{100}$ 9 $\frac{35}{100}$
10 $\frac{12}{100}$ 11 $\frac{96}{100}$ 12 $\frac{15}{100}$ 13 $\frac{84}{100}$ 14 $\frac{68}{100}$

Write and complete.

15 0.13 = $\frac{\square}{10}$ + $\frac{\square}{100}$ = $\frac{\square}{100}$ 16 0.74 = $\frac{\square}{10}$ + $\frac{\square}{100}$ = $\frac{\square}{100}$
17 0.81 = $\frac{\square}{10}$ + $\frac{\square}{100}$ = $\frac{\square}{100}$ 18 0.97 = $\frac{\square}{10}$ + $\frac{\square}{100}$ = $\frac{\square}{100}$
19 0.62 = $\frac{\square}{10}$ + $\frac{\square}{100}$ = $\frac{\square}{100}$ 20 0.55 = $\frac{\square}{10}$ + $\frac{\square}{100}$ = $\frac{\square}{100}$

Write as vulgar fractions (in hundredths).

21 0.17   22 0.26   23 0.85   24 0.42   25 0.51
26 0.34   27 0.59   28 0.66   29 0.73   30 0.38
31 0.89   32 0.23   33 0.99   34 0.41   35 0.22

E Q whole one or unit

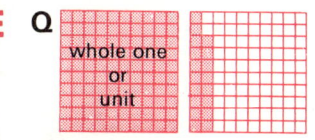

The shaded part in the diagram (Q) shows 1 whole one and 18 hundredths or 1.18

1 In the same way, write as decimals the shaded parts in these diagrams.

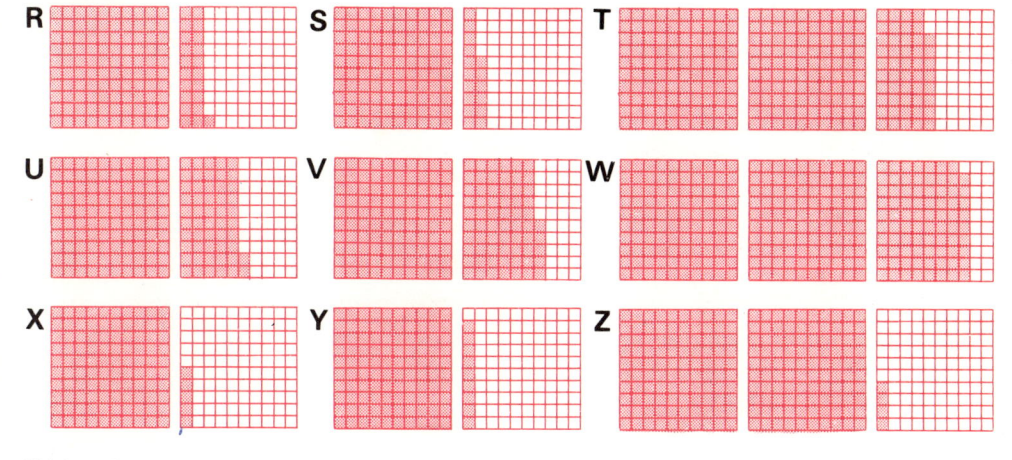

R   S   T

U   V   W

X   Y   Z

Write the number shown on each abacus picture as a decimal.

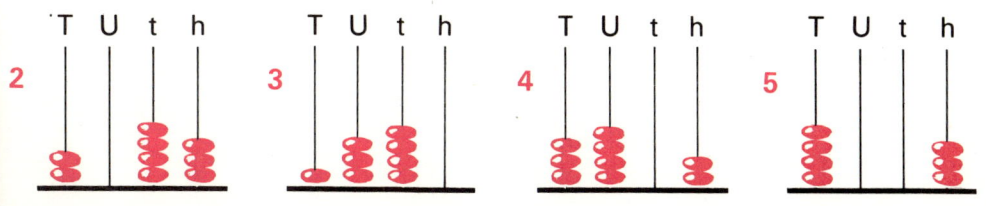

2   3   4   5

43

UNIT 21
Decimal fractions
notation tenths hundredths

A Draw abacus pictures to show these numbers.
1. 5.36
2. 4.15
3. 21.62
4. 36.5
5. 4.05
6. 50.61
7. 41.03
8. 10.0

Write each answer as a decimal.
9. $1 + \frac{3}{10} + \frac{7}{100}$
10. $2 + \frac{9}{10} + \frac{6}{100}$
11. $6 + \frac{4}{10} + \frac{5}{100}$
12. $9 + \frac{7}{10} + \frac{7}{10}$
13. $10 + \frac{6}{10} + \frac{4}{100}$
14. $15 + \frac{2}{10} + \frac{2}{100}$
15. $20 + 8 + \frac{15}{100}$
16. $30 + 6 + \frac{9}{10}$
17. $50 + 3 + \frac{26}{100}$
18. $43 + \frac{9}{100}$
19. $28 + \frac{8}{100}$
20. $10 + \frac{3}{100}$

Write and complete.
21. $1.29 = \square \text{unit} + \frac{\square}{10} + \frac{\square}{100} = \frac{\square}{10} + \frac{\square}{100} = \frac{\square}{100}$
22. $2.08 = \square \text{units} + \frac{\square}{100} = \frac{\square}{100}$
23. $3.62 = \frac{\square}{100}$
24. $4.05 = \frac{\square}{100}$
25. $5.23 = \frac{\square}{100}$
26. $8.08 = \frac{\square}{100}$

Write as decimals.
27. 26 hundredths
28. 58 hundredths
29. 34 hundredths
30. 195 hundredths
31. 213 hundredths
32. 102 hundredths
33. 307 hundredths
34. 1006 hundredths
35. 2005 hundredths

B Write the value of the figure underlined in each of these numbers.
1. 1_5_9
2. 51_9_
3. 591
4. 59.1
5. 59.0
6. 4_7_00
7. 400_7_
8. 26.8_2_
9. 262_8_
10. 26.2
11. 1_3_5.24
12. 1.5_3_
13. 1_3_.52
14. 1.7_8_
15. 1_7_8

Make each of these numbers 100 times bigger.
16. 0.75
17. 0.13
18. 0.64
19. 0.9
20. 1.87
21. 2.41
22. 1.36
23. 7.2
24. 1.07
25. 4.06
26. 7.07
27. 8.0
28. 0.2
29. 1.6
30. 10.5
31. 26

Make each of these numbers 100 times smaller.
32. 800
33. 500
34. 300
35. 10
36. 136
37. 285
38. 190
39. 41
40. 24
41. 69
42. 82
43. 71
44. 9
45. 7
46. 3
47. 5

C Arrange the following in order of size, the largest first.
1. 0.37 0.18 0.75 0.09 0.5
2. 3.0 1.81 0.99 2.07 1.60
3. 213.5 2.13 21.35 2135
4. 16.40 10.64 14.06 16.04 160.4

The large square represents a whole one or one unit.
Now write and complete the following.
5. $\frac{1}{2} = \frac{\square}{10} = \frac{\square}{100}$
6. $\frac{1}{4} = \frac{\square}{100}$
7. $\frac{3}{4} = \frac{\square}{100}$

Write as a decimal fraction.
8. $\frac{1}{2}$
9. $\frac{1}{4}$
10. $\frac{3}{4}$
11. $\frac{1}{10}$
12. $\frac{1}{5}$

D

Units	tenths	hundredths
£ 2	. 6	7

Write and complete.

1. £2·67 = £2 + £$\frac{\Box}{10}$ + £$\frac{\Box}{100}$ = £2 + £$\frac{\Box}{100}$ = £2 and □p
2. £4·89 = £4 + £$\frac{\Box}{10}$ + £$\frac{\Box}{100}$ = £□ + £$\frac{\Box}{100}$ = £□ and □p
3. £5·41 = £□ + £$\frac{\Box}{10}$ + £$\frac{\Box}{100}$ = £□ + £$\frac{\Box}{100}$ = £□ and □p
4. £8·40 = £□ + £$\frac{\Box}{10}$ = £□ and □pence
5. £6·90 = £□ + £$\frac{\Box}{10}$ = £□ and □pence
6. £7·06 = £□ + £$\frac{\Box}{100}$ = £□ and □pence

Write the value of each of the figures underlined.

7. £2·7<u>3</u>   8. £3·0<u>5</u>   9. £1<u>3</u>·19   10. £<u>16</u>·56
11. £11·1<u>0</u>   12. £17·<u>8</u>0   13. £24·<u>5</u>2   14. £2·<u>9</u>1

E

| 1p = £0·01 | 10p = £0·10 |

Write as £s
1. 5p   2. 3p   3. 8p   4. 2p   5. 4p
6. 60p   7. 50p   8. 2 TENS   9. 8 TENS   10. 7 TENS
11. 34p   12. 68p   13. 140p   14. 208p   15. 25 TENS

Multiply by 10
16. £2·00   17. £2·20   18. £1·50   19. £3·96   20. £1·68
21. £7·04   22. £0·07   23. £0·80   24. £10·40   25. £2·01

Divide by 10
26. £15   27. £25·00   28. £38·00   29. £3   30. £9·00
31. £1·50   32. £8·70   33. £23·20   34. £2·10   35. £4·30

Multiply by 100
1. £3   2. £6·00   3. £2·50   4. £1·70   5. £3·20
6. £1·10   7. £2·40   8. £1·20   9. £2·37   10. £4·58
11. £7·16   12. £1·89   13. £3·01   14. £5·04   15. £9·03

Divide by 100
16. £1·00   17. £4   18. £7·00   19. £9   20. £10·00
21. £40   22. £50·00   23. £80   24. £70·00   25. £30
26. £48·00   27. £26   28. £93·00   29. £62   30. £55·00

G

| 1 cm = 0·01 m | 10 cm = 0·10 m |

Write as metres
1. 2 cm   2. 5 cm   3. 6 cm   4. 9 cm   5. 7 cm
6. 30 cm   7. 60 cm   8. 90 cm   9. 80 cm   10. 40 cm
11. 52 cm   12. 26 cm   13. 48 cm   14. 256 cm   15. 391 cm

Write as cm
16. 0·34 m   17. 0·67 m   18. 0·52 m   19. 0·70 m   20. 0·50 m
21. 0·17 m   22. 3·40 m   23. 8·62 m   24. 9·21 m   25. 1·87 m

First find $\frac{1}{10}$ and then $\frac{7}{10}$ of
26. £0·10   27. £1·00   28. £10   29. £100   30. £1000
31. 0·10 m   32. 1·00 m   33. 10 m   34. 100 m   35. 1000 m.

First find $\frac{1}{100}$ and then $\frac{5}{100}$ of
36. £1   37. £10   38. £100   39. £1000   40. £10 000.

UNIT 22

Number, money, measures
multiplication and division

A Write the answers only when you can.
1. (3 × 4) + 2
2. (4 × 8) + 6
3. (8 × 9) + 5
4. (7 × 9) +
5. (5 × 5) + 4
6. (2 × 6) + 3
7. (3 × 6) + 4
8. (8 × 8) +
9. (7 × 8) + 6
10. (1 × 7) + 5
11. (6 × 8) + 7
12. (6 × 6) +
13. (6 × 3) + 2
14. (9 × 8) + 6
15. (0 × 4) + 3
16. (4 × 3) +
17. (9 × 7) + 6
18. (1 × 9) + 7
19. (4 × 9) + 8
20. (0 × 5) +

Write each of the following as a multiplication fact and work the answers
21. 5 sevens
22. 6 + 6 + 6 + 6
23. 9 + 9 + 9 + 9 + 9
24. six 8s
25. 7 + 7 + 7 + 7 + 7 + 7
26. 5 + 5 + 5 + 5
27. 9 threes
28. 3 + 3 + 3 + 3 + 3
29. 4 + 4 + 4 + 4 + 4 +
30. seven 7s
31. 2 + 2 + 2 + 2 + 2 + 2
32. 8 + 8 + 8 + 8

B
1. Find the value of the letter in each of the following.
   $a × 9 = 6 × 6$ $3 × b = 4 × 6$ $6 × 2 = c × 3$ $9 × 2 = 3 ×$
   $e × 10 = 8 × 5$ $2 × f = 4 × 4$ $4 × 5 = g × 10$ $5 × 2 = 10 ×$
   $i × 10 = 6 × 5$ $3 × 7 = k × 3$ $6 × 9 = m × 6$ $7 × 8 = n ×$
   $p × 2 = 2 × 7$ $q × 5 = 5 × 8$ $r × 4 = 4 × 2$

Write the answers only.
2. 40 × 8
3. 60 × 7
4. 50 × 9
5. 30 × 8
6. 2 × 7
7. 3 × 80
8. 4 × 90
9. 3 × 120
10. 20 × 9
11. 50 ×
12. 70 × 6
13. 130 × 7

C Find the cost of

1. 4 kg at 70p per kg
2. 3½ kg at 95p per ½ kg
3. 9 kg at £0·46 per kg
4. 500 g at £0·65 per 100 g
5. 700 g at £0·38 per 200 g

6. 4 m at 77p per ½ m
7. 2½ m at 52p per ½ m
8. 7 m at £1.28 per m
9. 9 m at £2·75 per m
10. 6 m at £4·53 per m

11. 1½ litres at 58p per ½ litre
12. 5 litres at 19p per litre
13. 7 litres at 7p per ½ litre
14. 2 litres at 6p per 200 mℓ
15. 1½ litres at 10p per 200 mℓ

16. 3 m at 20p per 10 cm
17. 2½ m at 75p per 50 cm
18. 5 m at 40p per 25 cm
19. 1¼ m at £1·30 per 25 cm
20. 1.5 m at £0·20 per 20 cm.

D Multiply by 10.
1. 6.4 cm
2. 2.34 m
3. 1.65 m
4. 2.75 kg
5. 0.5 litres
6. 2.4 km
7. 3.02 m
8. 0.25 kg
9. 0.8 kg
10. 3.9 litres
11. 11.5 m
12. 24.8 cm
13. 20.75 kg
14. 58.2 kg
15. 10.5 litr

Multiply by 100.
16. £2·53
17. 3.76 m
18. 8.75 kg
19. 6.25 m
20. 2.08 litr
21. £7·20
22. 4.95 m
23. £0·95
24. 0.52 m
25. 0.75 litr
26. 5.5 kg
27. 2.7 km
28. 9.5 kg
29. 1.8 litres
30. 0.6 litres

E Write the answers only. Each has a remainder.

1 5)47	2 7)39	3 9)84	4 3)31	5 6)52
6 8)75	7 4)23	8 7)69	9 5)29	10 9)25
11 6)65	12 3)29	13 8)43	14 4)39	15 7)33
16 9)52	17 6)33	18 5)19	19 8)60	20 4)15

F Write each of the examples **1–5** as a division fact and write the answer to each example.
1. 36 sweets shared equally between 4 boys. How many each?
2. 54p divided equally among 9 girls. How much each?
3. 35 cakes placed in equal groups of 5. How many groups?
4. 48 cards wrapped in packets of 6. How many packets?
5. 18 litres in bottles each holding 2 litres. How many bottles?

A tin holds 4 kg of toffees and each toffee has a mass of 10 g.
6. How many toffees are there in the tin?

If the toffees are wrapped in packets, how many packets will there be if the sweets are in packets of
7 5   8 4   9 8   10 10?

G Write the value of the letter in each of the following.
1. $56 \div 7 = 24 \div a$ $12 \div 4 = 27 \div b$ $63 \div 9 = 42 \div c$
   $54 \div d = 18 \div 3$ $72 \div e = 45 \div 5$ $40 \div f = 24 \div 3$
   $36 \div 6 = 30 \div g$ $64 \div 8 = 32 \div h$ $48 \div 6 = 16 \div j$

Write the answers only.

Divide by 4	2 24 g	3 240 g	4 2.400 kg	5 24.000 kg
Divide by 8	6 32 mℓ	7 320 mℓ	8 3.200 litres	9 32.000 litres
Divide by 7	10 49 mm	11 490 mm	12 4.900 m	13 49.000 m
Divide by 9	14 72 g	15 720 g	16 7.200 kg	17 72.000 kg
Divide by 6	18 54 mℓ	19 540 mℓ	20 5.400 litres	21 54.000 litres

H

Find the cost of **1 kg** if
1 5 kg cost 60p
2 9 kg cost £3·06
3 8 kg cost £0·64
4 7 kg cost £20·09
5 6 kg cost £3

Find the cost of **1 m** if
6 8 m cost £1·28
7 5 m cost £29
8 4 m cost £20·20
9 7 m cost £8·19
10 6 m cost £12·42

I Divide by 10.

1 £28	2 56 cm	3 42 km	4 35 kg	5 23 m
6 64 cm	7 250 km	8 110 cm	9 96 m	10 75 kg
11 £2·10	12 5 litres	13 2.5 litres	14 8.7 m	15 7.5 kg

Divide by 100.

16 725 litres	17 420 kg	18 £24	19 18 litres	20 35 kg
21 50 kg	22 20 m	23 65 km	24 150 litres	25 1000 km
26 £20	27 15 m	28 £6	29 4 m	30 975 m

UNIT 23
Shapes   quadrilaterals

A   **A reminder**   **Shapes with 4 sides are called quadrilaterals.**

The following shapes are special kinds of quadrilaterals.

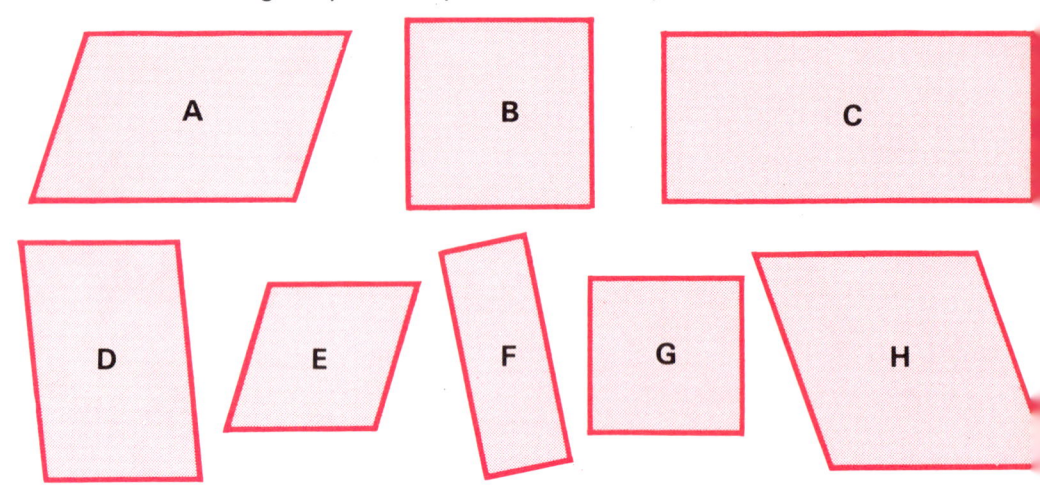

Measure the sides and test the angles with the right angle of a set square.

Then write the letter of each shape in which there are
1   4 right angles
2   no right angles
3   2 acute angles and 2 obtuse angles
4   4 equal sides
5   2 sides which are perpendicular to the base
6   2 pairs of parallel equal sides.

Which of the quadrilaterals are
7   squares
8   rectangles
9   rhombuses
10   parallelograms

B   Using a ruler and set square, construct the following shapes.
1   square M, sides 6.5 cm long
2   square N, sides 43 mm long
3   square O, sides 10.7 cm long
4   rectangle P, length 7.5 cm, breadth 3.0 cm
5   rectangle Q, length 38 mm, width 50 mm
6   rectangle R, length 93 mm, breadth 2.6 cm

Find the perimeter of each shape. Write the answers
7   as cm and mm
8   as mm.

In each shape draw two diagonals and measure them in mm.
Are the diagonals equal in
9   each square
10   each rectangle?

Find by measuring if the diagonals bisect each other in
11   each square
12   each rectangle.

Write and complete.
13   The diagonals of a square and a rectangle are _____ in length and _____ each other.

C

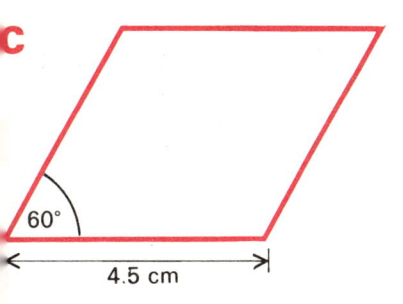

1 Using a ruler and set square construct a rhombus to the given measurements.
Find the perimeter of the rhombus in
2 cm   3 mm.
Draw two diagonals in the rhombus and find by measuring if
4 they are equal   5 they bisect each other.

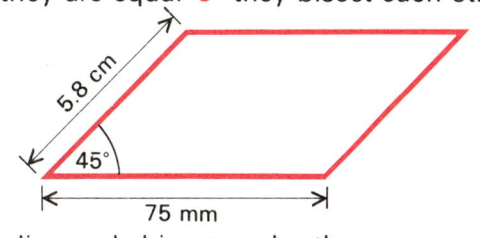

(rhombus: 4.5 cm side, 60°)
(parallelogram: 5.8 cm, 75 mm, 45°)

Now draw a parallelogram to the given measurements.
Find its perimeter in
6 mm   7 cm.
Find by measuring if
8 the diagonals are equal   9 the diagonals bisect each other.

10 Draw a rhombus Y and a parallelogram Z using the given measurements. 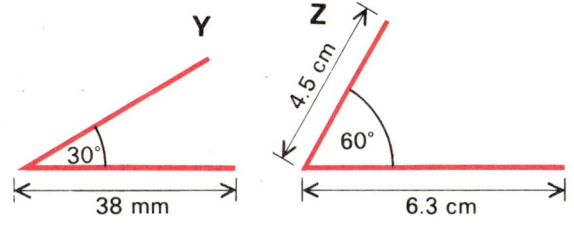
Find the perimeter of each shape
11 in mm   12 in cm.
Find for each shape if
13 the diagonals are equal   14 the diagonals bisect each other.

(Y: 38 mm, 30°)
(Z: 4.5 cm, 6.3 cm, 60°)

D

A reminder   The four angles of any quadrilateral together equal 4 right angles or 360°.

1 In each of the quadrilaterals find in degrees the size of the angle marked x.

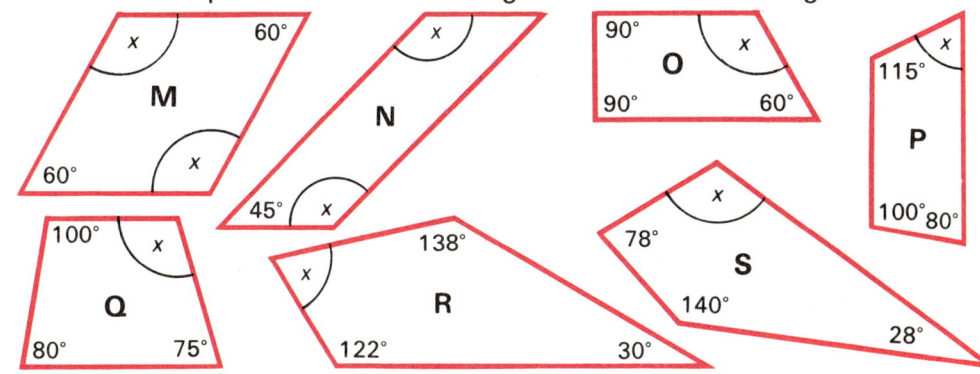

M: x, 60°, 60°, x
N: x, 45°, x, 138°, 122°
O: 90°, x, 90°, 60°
P: x, 115°, 100°, 80°
Q: 100°, x, 80°, 75°
R: x, 138°, 122°
S: x, 78°, 140°, 28°

Write the letter of each shape which has
2 2 pairs of parallel sides (give the special name of each shape)
3 1 pair of parallel sides   4 no parallel sides.
5 A shape with only **one pair** of parallel sides has a special name — **a trapezium**. Which of the shapes above are trapeziums?
6 Draw three trapeziums T, U, V, each of a different size.
7 Measure, in mm, the sides of each and find the perimeters in cm.
8 Draw the diagonals in each trapezium.
Find by measuring if
9 the diagonals are equal   10 the diagonals bisect each other.

49

UNIT 24

Plans   drawing to scale

A   **Plans show the shape of objects when looked at from above.**

1   Draw plans, full size, of each of these objects, the measurements of which are given.

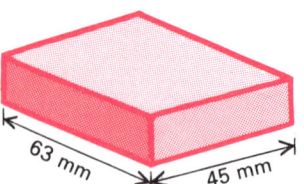

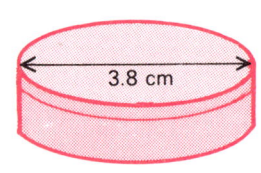

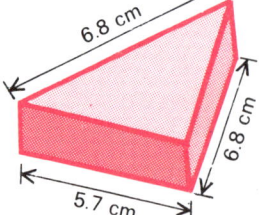

2   In each drawing the measurement of the height is not given. Give the reason.

B   The drawings show the plans of three boxes of different shapes.

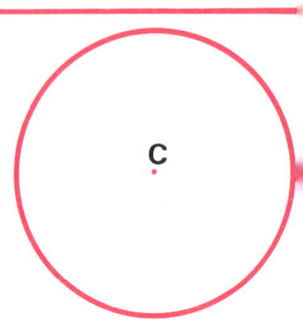

Measure in mm
1   the length and breadth of plan A   2   the length and breadth of plan B
3   the diameter of plan C.

The measurements of plan A are drawn $\frac{1}{2}$ the actual size.
4   Find the actual length and breadth of the box in mm; in cm.
Write and complete.
5   Plan A is drawn to the scale   1 mm to □ mm   or   1 cm to □ cm.

The measurements of plan B are drawn $\frac{1}{5}$ the actual size.
6   Find the actual length and breadth of the box in mm; in cm.
Write and complete.
7   Plan B is drawn to the scale   1 mm to □ mm   or   1 cm to □ cm.

The measurements of plan C are drawn $\frac{1}{10}$ the actual size.
8   Find the actual length of the diameter and the radius in mm; in cm.
Write and complete.
9   Plan C is drawn to the scale   1 mm to □ mm   or   1 cm to □ cm.

C   The line VW is drawn to the scale 1 cm to 4 cm.
V ——————————————————— W
1   Measure the line VW in cm and find the length it represents.
2   What fraction of the actual length is the line VW?

> The scale 1 cm to 4 cm can be expressed as the fraction $\frac{1}{4}$.
> It can also be expressed as a ratio in this way 1 : 4.

Express each of these scales as a fraction; as a ratio.
3   1 cm to 2 cm   4   1 mm to 5 mm   5   1 cm to 10 c
6   1 cm to 20 cm   7   1 m to 25 m   8   1 cm to 50 c

D 1 By measuring and using the scale, find the actual length represented by each of these lines. Give the answers, first in cm and then in m.

a ———————————————— Scale 1 cm to 20 cm
b ———————————————————— Scale 1 cm to 50 cm
c —————————— Scale 1 cm to 100 cm (1 metre)
d ———————————————————————— Scale 1 cm to 500 cm (5 m)
e ——————————— Scale 1 mm to 10 mm (1 cm)
f ———————————————— Scale 1 mm to 50 mm (5 cm)
g ———————————————————————————— Scale 1 mm to 100 mm (10 cm)

2 Write each of the scales as a fraction; as a ratio.

3 The drawings show the plans of two plots of land X and Y.
Using tracing paper, copy each plan.

X
Scale 1 cm to 5 m
(1:500)

Y
Scale 1 cm to 10 m
(1:1000)

4 Measure the sides on each of the plans and show the actual lengths in metres on the tracings.

5 Find the perimeter of each plot in metres.

E Using the scale
1 cm to 10 cm (1:10), draw lines to represent
1 50 cm   **2** 85 cm   **3** 74 cm   **4** 1 metre.
1 cm to 1 metre (1:100), draw lines to represent
5 7 m   **6** $4\frac{1}{2}$ m   **7** 9.5 m   **8** 8.7 m.
1 cm to 10 m (1:1000), draw lines to represent
9 60 m   **10** 100 m   **11** 75 m   **12** 103 m.
1 mm to 5 cm (1:50), draw lines to represent
13 100 cm   **14** 3 m   **15** 650 cm.

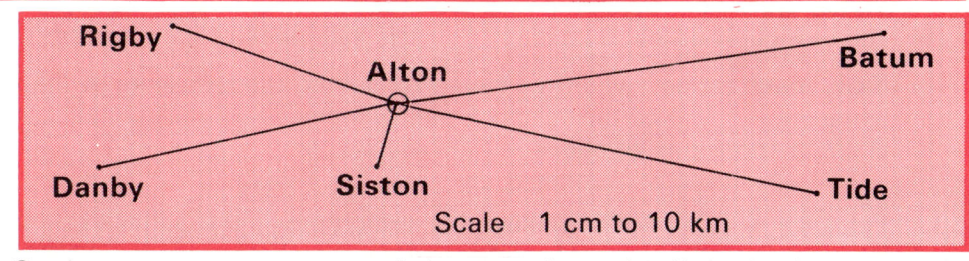

F

Rigby
Alton
Batum
Danby
Siston
Tide
Scale   1 cm to 10 km

On the map, measure accurately in cm and mm the distances from Alton to
1 Batum   **2** Tide   **3** Siston   **4** Danby   **5** Rigby.
6 Use the scale to find the actual distances in km.
Find the actual distances 'as the crow flies' between
7 Rigby and Batum   **8** Danby and Tide.
Using the scale 1 cm to 1 km draw lines which represent
9 14 km   **10** 9.7 km   **11** 4.5 km   **12** 6.3 km.
13 Express the scale 1 cm to 1 km first as a fraction then as a ratio.

UNIT 25
Shopping   costing items

A
1. Check the supermarket bills **a** and **b** to make sure that each total is correct

a	b	c	d	e
00·05	00·06	00·19	00·17	00·13
00·18	00·10	00·27	00·09	01·27
00·25	00·58	00·04	00·23	00·06
01·66	01·07	00·37	00·34	00·43
02·04	00·62	00·26	00·07	00·07
£04·18 T	£02·43 T	01·44	00·56	00·02
		00·52	00·26	00·77
				00·09
				00·13

2. Now find the total of each of the bills **c**, **d** and **e**.
3. Name the coins, using as few as possible, which are required to pay each of the five bills.
4. Find the change if each bill is paid with a £5 note.
5. Make up similar bills of at least 8 items and find their totals. Ask a partner to check each total.

B
The prices of articles of children's clothing are given in the table.

cardigan	jeans	shirt	shoes	tie	gloves	socks
£4·16	£10·08	£6·52	£14·80	£1·52	£2·60	96p

Find the total cost of
1. 1 cardigan, 1 pair of shoes, 1 shirt
2. 1 pair of jeans, 1 pair of gloves, 2 ties.
3. As a special offer 3 pairs of socks can be bought for £2·60. How much is saved by buying 3 pairs?

At the New Year Sale all prices are reduced by $\frac{1}{4}$. Find
4. the reduction on each article   5. the sale price of each article.

How much money would be saved by buying the following at the sale?
6. 2 ties   7. 1 cardigan and 1 pair of jeans
8. 3 shirts and 1 pair of shoes.

C
For each of the following examples, which buy is the better value for money? Give the reason for your choice.
1. a Detergent at 29p for each bottle   or
   b a bottle holding 3 times as much for 80p.
2. a Envelopes at 25 for 44p   or   b packets of 10 costing 20p.
3. a Potatoes at 9p per $\frac{1}{2}$ kg   or   b a 5 kg bag for 85p.
4. a Orange squash at $\frac{1}{2}$ litre for 28p   or   b a 250 mℓ bottle for 13p.
5. a Biscuits at 48p for a $\frac{1}{2}$ kg box   or   b 200 g packets at 24p each.

What fraction of 1 metre is
1. 50 cm 2. 75 cm 3. 10 cm 4. 30 cm 5. 70 cm?

10 cm of material cost 35p. Find the cost of
6. 20 cm 7. 30 cm 8. 50 cm 9. 80 cm 10. 1 metre.

1 metre of ribbon costs 40p. Find the cost of
11. 3 m 12. 50 cm 13. 10 cm 14. 30 cm 15. 70 cm 16. 90 cm.

Find the cost of
17. 2 m 20 cm at 15p per metre   18. 4 m 25 cm at 48p per metre
19. 1 m 60 cm at 35p per metre   20. 5 m 40 cm at 75p per metre.

21. A shopkeeper sells different kinds of materials at the given prices per metre. Draw and fill in this ready reckoner.

price per metre	10 cm	20 cm	30 cm	40 cm	50 cm	60 cm	70 cm	80 cm	90 cm
70p									
£1·20									
£2·50									

Check the ready reckoner from the answer book and correct any mistakes.

Using the ready reckoner find the cost of
22. 60 cm at £1·20 per m   23. 90 cm at £2·50 per m
24. 2 m 30 cm at 70p per m   25. 3 m 80 cm at £1·20 per m.

26. Make up similar shopping items and find their cost using the ready reckoner.

What fraction of 1 kg is
1. 500 g 2. 250 g 3. 750 g 4. 100 g 5. 300 g 6. 700 g?

100 g cost 8p. Find the cost of
7. ½ kg 8. 1 kg 9. 200 g 10. 600 g 11. 900 g.

Find the cost of each of the following at 7p per 100 g.
12. ½ kg 13. 1 kg 14. 300 g 15. 700 g 16. 900 g

1 kg costs 80p.   Find the cost of 17. 500 g 18. 100 g 19. 600 g.
1 kg costs £1·20. Find the cost of 20. ½ kg   21. 100 g 22. 300 g.
½ kg costs 30p.   Find the cost of 23. 100 g 24. 400 g 25. 1 kg.
½ kg costs 45p.   Find the cost of 26. 100 g 27. 300 g 28. 700 g.

Draw and fill in this ready reckoner. Then check it and correct any mistakes.

Use it to find the cost of
2. 700 g at 80p per kg
3. 400 g at 90p per kg
4. 600 g at 60p per kg
5. 1 kg 300 g at 90p per kg
6. 2 kg 200 g at 80p per kg
7. 3 kg 800 g at 60p per kg.

8. Make up similar shopping items and find their cost using the ready reckoner.

mass	cost per kg		
	60p	80p	90p
100 g			
200 g			
300 g			
400 g			
500 g (½ kg)			
600 g			
700 g			
800 g			
900 g			

UNIT 26

Looking back

A Turn back to **Unit 6** and work **F1–30**, **G1–30** and **H1–30** as quickly as possible.

B Write and complete these number series.
1 10 000, 1000, 100, ☐, ☐, ☐
2 5000, 500, 50, ☐, ☐, ☐
3 0.02, 0.2, 2, ☐, ☐, ☐
4 0.6, 6, 60, ☐, ☐, ☐
5 0.01, 1, ☐, ☐, 1 000 000

Write the **decimal fraction** of each shape which is
6 shaded
7 unshaded.

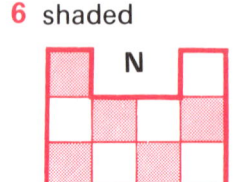

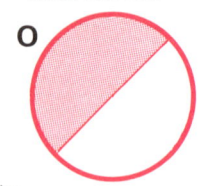

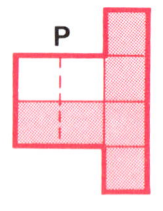

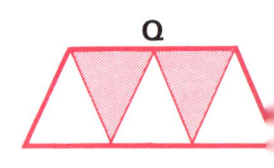

Write and complete.
8 ☐mm = 1 cm
9 ☐cm = 1 m
10 ☐mm = 1 m
11 ☐m = 1 km
12 0.1 cm = ☐mm
13 0.01 m = ☐cm
14 0.001 m = ☐mm
15 0.001 km = ☐m

C 1 Measure and then write in **mm** the length of each of these lines.
a
b
c
d
e

Write in **cm** the length of a line **10 times** as long as
2 line a
3 line b
4 line c
5 line d
6 line e

Write in **m** the length of a line **100 times** as long as
7 line a
8 line b
9 line c
10 line d
11 line e

D The diagram shows the distances between some villages.

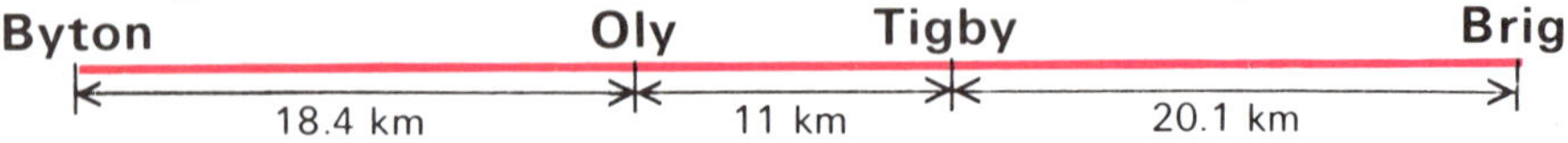

Byton — 18.4 km — Oly — 11 km — Tigby — 20.1 km — Brig

At Byton the reading on a bus odometer is 1170.6 km.
Write the reading which will be shown when it reaches
1 Oly
2 Tigby
3 Brig.

bus timetable						
	Byton	11.35	12.00	12.25	12.50	13.15
	Oly	12.12	12.37	13.02	13.27	13.52
	Tigby	12.36	13.01	13.26	13.51	14.16
	Brig	13.16	13.41	14.06	14.31	14.56

How long does each bus take from Byton to
4 Oly
5 Tigby
6 Brig?
7 How often do the buses depart from Byton?
Which is the first bus that can be caught from
8 Byton after half past 12
9 Oly after 1.30 p.m.
10 Tigby after quarter to
11 Byton after 11.45 a.m.
12 Oly after mid-day
13 Tigby after $\frac{1}{4}$ past 1?

The chart shows how many of the different kinds of coins were saved by classes 1 to 4.

class	1p	2p	5p	10p	20p
1	28	46	52	20	7
2	18	30	37	24	5
3	23	32	40	28	6
4	19	36	35	32	9

Find the total amount saved in
1. 1p coins   2. TWOS
3. FIVES   4. TENS   5. TWENTIES.
6. Find the amount saved altogether.
7. Write in order, the total amount saved by each class, the largest amount first.

Each line in this drawing is named by a letter.
Name the lines which are
1. horizontal   2. vertical   3. oblique.
Name the line or lines parallel to
4. line P   5. line Q   6. line M   7. line R.

The measurements of some angles are given below.

| 30° | 150° | 90° | 135° | 60° |

Which of the angles
8. are acute angles   9. are obtuse angles   10. is a right angle?

Look at the angles drawn below.
Without measuring, write the letter of the angle which is
11. 30°   12. 150°   13. 90°   14. 135°   15. 60°.

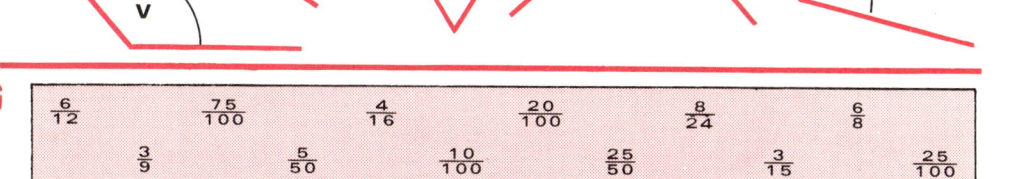

$\frac{6}{12}$ $\frac{75}{100}$ $\frac{4}{16}$ $\frac{20}{100}$ $\frac{8}{24}$ $\frac{6}{8}$
$\frac{3}{9}$ $\frac{5}{50}$ $\frac{10}{100}$ $\frac{25}{50}$ $\frac{3}{15}$ $\frac{25}{100}$

Write two fractions from the box each of which is equal in value to
1. $\frac{1}{2}$ 2. $\frac{1}{4}$ 3. $\frac{3}{4}$ 4. $\frac{1}{3}$ 5. $\frac{1}{5}$ 6. $\frac{1}{10}$.

How many
7. halves in $10\frac{1}{2}$ 8. thirds in $4\frac{2}{3}$ 9. quarters in $3\frac{3}{4}$ 10. fifths in $5\frac{2}{5}$
11. sixths in $2\frac{5}{6}$ 12. tenths in $6\frac{7}{10}$?

Find $\frac{1}{5}$ and then $\frac{3}{5}$ of
13. £3·65   14. 800 g   15. 965 mℓ   16. 690 m   17. 150 kg.

Find $\frac{3}{8}$ of
18. £48   19. 64 mm   20. 96 kg   21. 72 litres   22. 56 km
23. 88 cm   24. £32   25. 400 litres   26. 144 km   27. 120 kg.

Find the sum of
28. 2^2 and 3^2 29. 4^2 and 4^2 30. 5^2 and 1^2 31. 6^2 and 7^2.

Find the difference between
32. 8^2 and 4^2 33. 9^2 and 3^2 34. 10^2 and 5^2 35. 7^2 and 2^2.

55

UNIT 27

Shapes triangles

A

> **A reminder** A triangle has 3 sides and 3 angles.

Triangles are named according to their sides.

Measure the sides of each triangle in mm. Then write the letter of the triangles which are
1 **equilateral** (3 equal sides)
2 **isosceles** (2 equal sides)
3 **scalene** (no equal sides).

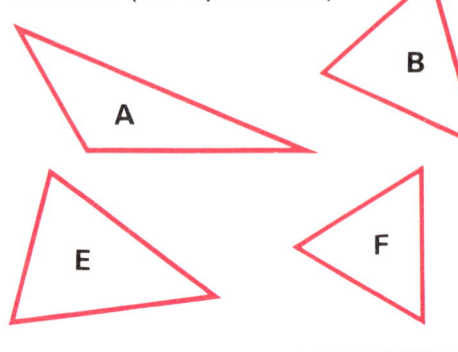

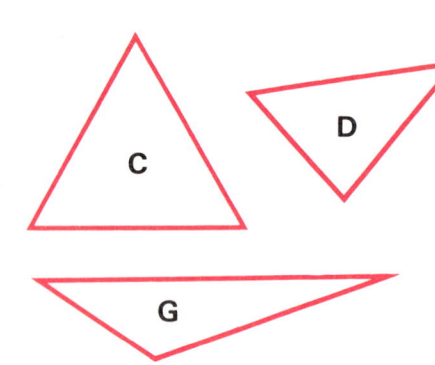

B Triangles are named according to their angles.

Use a set square to find which of the triangles below are
1 right-angled
2 acute-angled
3 obtuse-angled triangles

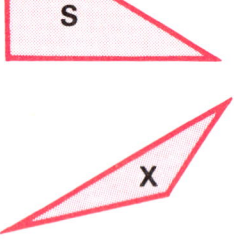

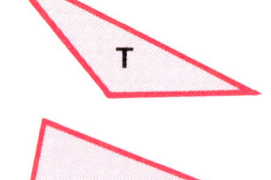

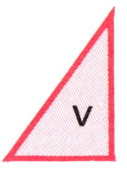

C

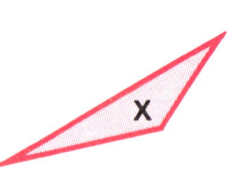

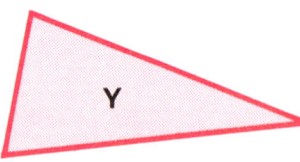

In the triangle ABC name
1 the line which is the base
2 the point which is the vertex.
3 Measure in mm the length of the sides BC, BA, CA.
4 Use a ruler and compasses to construct the triangle ABC as shown.

5 In the same way draw these triangles having sides measuring
K 105 mm   70 mm   55 mm   L 6.5 cm   8.5 cm   3.0 cm
M 75 mm   60 mm   45 mm   N 3.8 cm   5.6 cm   4.8 cm.

Name each triangle you have drawn
6 according to the sides
7 according to the angles.

Use a ruler and compasses to draw four equilateral triangles the sides of which measure
1. 5.5 cm
2. 73 mm
3. 46 mm
4. 6.2 cm.
5. With a set square, measure the three angles in each triangle.

Write and complete.
6. The angles of an equilateral triangle each measure ☐°.

Construct four isosceles triangles the sides of which measure
7. base 45 mm   two equal sides of 60 mm
8. base 6.4 cm   two equal sides of 5.3 cm
9. base 76 mm   two equal sides of 42 mm
10. base 5.8 cm   two equal sides of 7.0 cm.
11. Mark with a letter 'x' the angles in each triangle which are opposite the equal sides.
12. Write what you know about the angles opposite the equal sides in an isosceles triangle.

A reminder   The sum of the three angles of a triangle is 180°.

1. Find the size in degrees of each angle marked x.

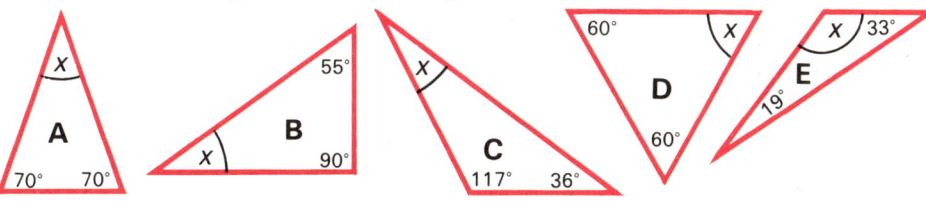

   A: 70°, 70°, x
   B: 55°, 90°, x
   C: 117°, 36°, x
   D: 60°, 60°, x
   E: 19°, 33°, x

2. Name each triangle according to its sides.

The size of each of two angles in a triangle is given in the table.

3. Calculate the size of the third angle.

Name each triangle according to
4. its angles   5. its sides.

triangle	angles		
W	34°	56°	
X	60°		60°
Y	27°		35°
Z	59°	59°	

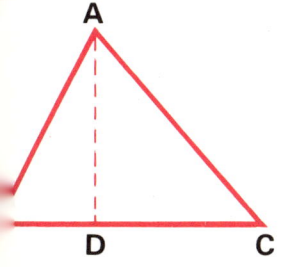

In the triangle ABC, measure in mm
1. the base BC
2. the perpendicular height AD
3. Measure in mm the other two sides of the triangle.
4. Now draw the triangle so that AB is the base.
5. Measure the perpendicular height of the triangle.

In the triangle XYZ measure in mm
6. the base YZ   7. the perpendicular height XP.
8. Measure in mm the other two sides of the triangle.
9. Now draw the triangle so that XZ is the base.
10. Measure the perpendicular height.

Use a ruler and set square to draw and measure in mm the perpendicular height of each triangle in **D1–4** and **D7–10**.

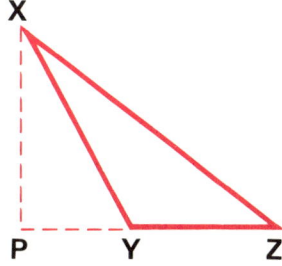

57

UNIT 28
Number and money four rules

A 1   3801
       4070
    + 1016

2   1100
     404
  + 5302

3   3056
    1204
  + 740

4   1540
    3258
  + 2002

5   £
   3·16
   0·08
   4·03
 + 1·50

6   £
  23·28
   6·35
  10·03
+ 40·26

7   £
  32·24
   1·08
   6·00
+ 20·39

8   £
   2·45
  26·05
   0·3
+ 11·1

9   1372
    189
    376
 + 263

10 1223
   2074
    555
 + 1048

11 1537
    163
   2009
 + 736

12 3080
   214
    55
 + 167

13 £
   4·48
  36·00
   0·36
+ 50·15

14 £
  27·02
  10·43
   8·50
+ 32·04

15 £
  23·96
   7·38
  15·44
+ 10·70

16 £
  18·4
  12·9
  29·7
+ 31·3

```
U         V         W                   X
|←138 km→|←109 km→|←─── 283 km ───→|←97 km→|
```

The diagram above shows the distances between five towns U, V, W, X and Y. How far is it from

17 U to W   18 V to X   19 W to Y   20 Y to V   21 X to U   22 Y to U

B 1 £
   12·86
  − 1·70

2 £
  25·34
− 15·01

3 £
  49·84
− 30·02

4 £
  70·2
− 30·1

5 3850
 − 1126

6 4970
 − 388

7 6407
 − 2335

8 306
 − 252

9 £
  15·03
 − 7·82

10 £
  50·87
− 26·84

11 £
  30·54
 − 5·20

12 £
 100·0
 − 36·7

13 3755
 − 1867

14 1222
 − 346

15 8725
 − 1939

16 492
 − 196

Draw and complete these number squares. In each square, each row, column and diagonal must add up to the same total.

17
80	90	130
		50
70		

18
	17	83
	62	
41	107	

19
184		209
	188	
		192

20
		29
	333	
371		28

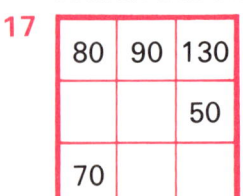

C
1. 132 × 2
2. 31 × 5
3. 63 × 3
4. 42 × 4
5. 27 × 8
6. 62 × 9
7. 46 × 7
8. 93 × 6

9. £0·48 × 3
10. £0·75 × 5
11. £0·62 × 9
12. £0·37 × 7

13. 180 × 2
14. 370 × 6
15. 240 × 8
16. 450 × 4

17. £0·06 × 9
18. £0·04 × 6
19. £5·08 × 7
20. £9·03 × 8

21. £4·01 × 4
22. £9·03 × 3
23. £6·04 × 2
24. £9·02 × 4

25. 975 × 5
26. 624 × 8
27. 973 × 7
28. 852 × 9

29. 9 classes each of 35 children. How many children altogether?
30. 7 rows of 18 chairs. How many chairs altogether?
31. What number is 6 times greater than 154?
32. Find by multiplying 185 + 185 + 185 + 185.
33. $\frac{1}{8}$ of a sum of money is £8·32. What is the sum of money?

D
1. 2)196
2. 5)235
3. 7)1491
4. 9)2943
5. 8)£3·44
6. 6)£4·56
7. 4)£16·56
8. 3)£26·55
9. 9)1440
10. 5)1350
11. 8)1520
12. 6)5100
13. 2)£0·68
14. 7)£0·91
15. 8)£0·64
16. 9)£0·54
17. 5)1143
18. 4)2871
19. 6)2000
20. 8)3782
21. 7)£8·82
22. 6)£15·48
23. 9)£43·65
24. 8)£103·44
25. 7)£98·07
26. 6)£54·24
27. 3)£45·27
28. 9)£108·18

29. How many pencils each costing 6p can be bought for £2·82?
30. 4 classes each contain 36 children. If all the children are placed in six equal classes, how many children will there be in each class?
31. A list of 60 names is to be written in 4 equal columns. How many names will there be in each column?

UNIT 29

Area squares and rectangles

A | **A reminder** | The amount of surface in a shape is called its **area**. Area is measured in square units of the same size.

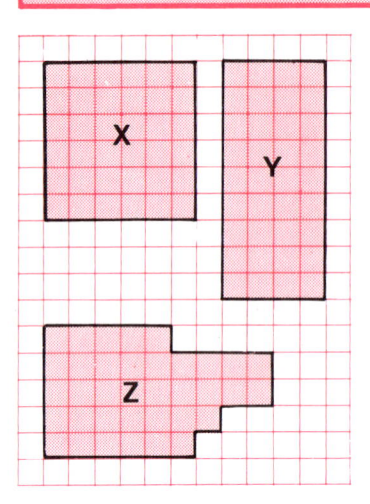

The surface of each shape X, Y and Z has been covered with square units.

1 Count the squares. What do you discover about the area of each shape?

> **Different shapes can have the same area.**

On squared paper draw

2 a square and a rectangle each with an area of 16 square units

3 three rectangles of different shape each with an area of 24 square units

4 three different shapes, not rectangles, each with an area of 20 square units.

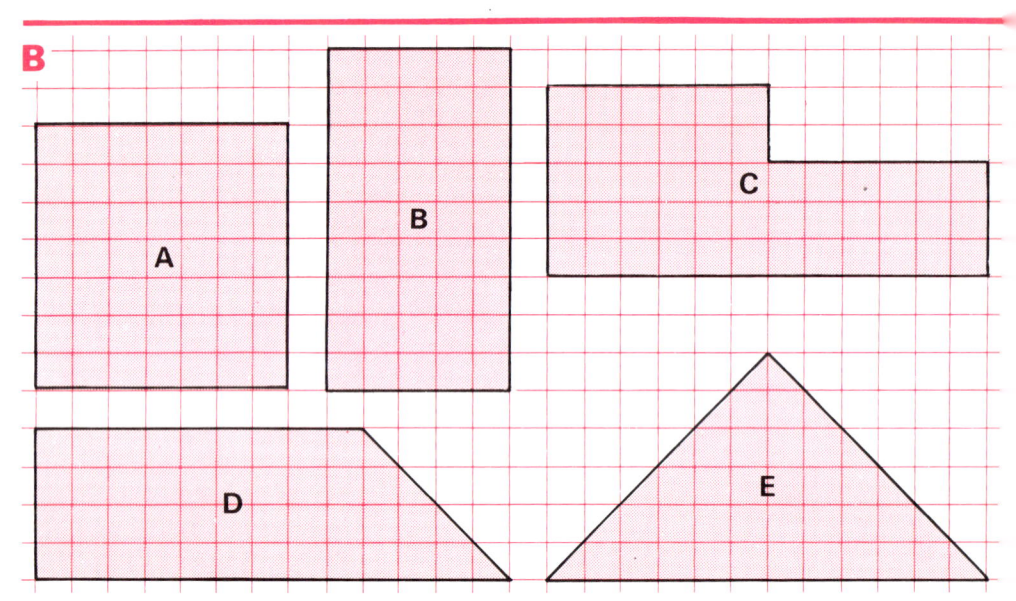

B

1 By counting find the area of each shape in square units. Notice that in some cases there are half-units to be counted.

Which shape has
2 the largest area
3 the smallest area?

4 Write the shapes in order putting the one with the smallest area first.

On ½ cm squared paper, draw
5 a rectangle with the same area as shape C
6 a rectangle which has an area twice that of shape B
7 a square equal in area to triangle E
8 a triangle equal in area to square A.

C When the sides of a square or rectangle are measured in cm the area is measured in square centimetres (cm²).

Measure in cm
1. the length
2. the breadth of the rectangle.

Its surface is covered with square centimetres.
3. How many cm² are there in one row?
4. How many rows?
5. How many cm² are there altogether?

Write and complete.
6. Area = (7 × 5) cm² = ☐ cm²

D In the diagram below
1. Measure the length and breadth of shape A.
2. What is the name of this shape?
Find its area by writing and completing
3. Area = (☐ × ☐) cm² = ☐ cm².

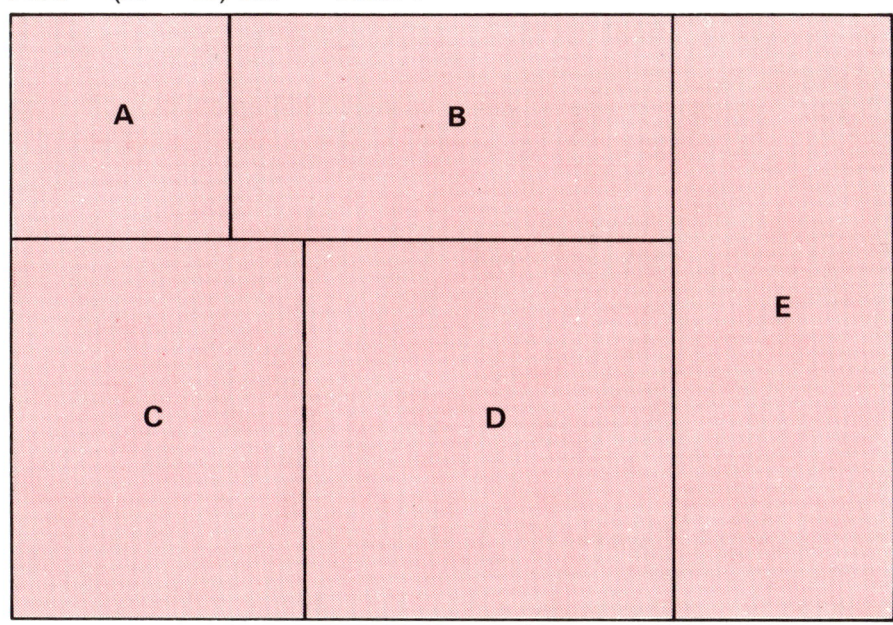

In the same way for each of the shapes B, C, D and E
4. measure the sides   5. name the shape   6. find the area.

Measure and find the area of the large rectangle formed
7. by A, B, C and D   8. by A, B, C, D and E.
Check your answers by adding the small areas.

The measurements of some squares and rectangles are given. Find the area of each.
9. length and width 9 cm
10. length 14 cm, breadth 9 cm
11. length 16 cm, width 7 cm
12. length and width 20 cm
13. length 18½ cm, breadth 8 cm
14. length 24 cm, width 3½ cm
15. length 40 cm, width 7½ cm
16. length 100 cm, breadth 50 cm

61

UNIT 30

Area
squares, rectangles, irregular shapes

A Three sheets of cardboard are marked A, B and C.
Sheet A measures 18 cm long and 6 cm wide.
Sheet B measures 20 cm by $4\frac{1}{2}$ cm.
Sheet C measures 12 cm × 9.5 cm.

1 Find the area of each sheet of cardboard.
2 By how many cm² is the area of the largest sheet greater than that of the smallest?
3 A rectangle measures 17.5 cm by 4 cm. Find its perimeter and its area.
4 If the length and breadth of the rectangle were doubled, find its perimeter and its area.

The perimeter of a square is 32 cm. Find
5 the length of one side   **6** the area of the square.

The diagram shows the dimensions of a piece of metal. 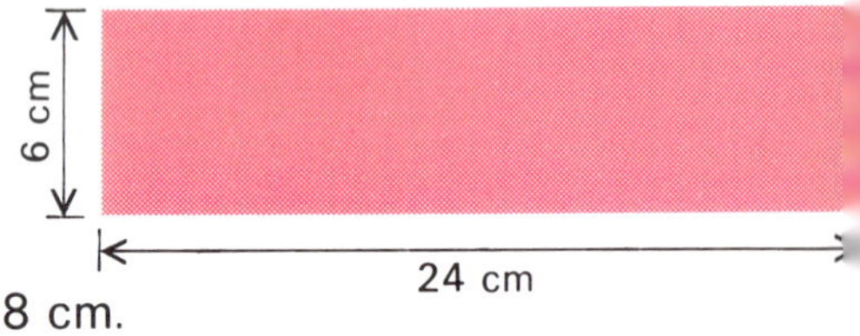
7 How many strips 2 cm wide can be cut from it?
8 Find the total length of the strips.
9 The side of a square tile measures 8 cm.
If 9 tiles were placed side by side in a row, what area would they cover?

B

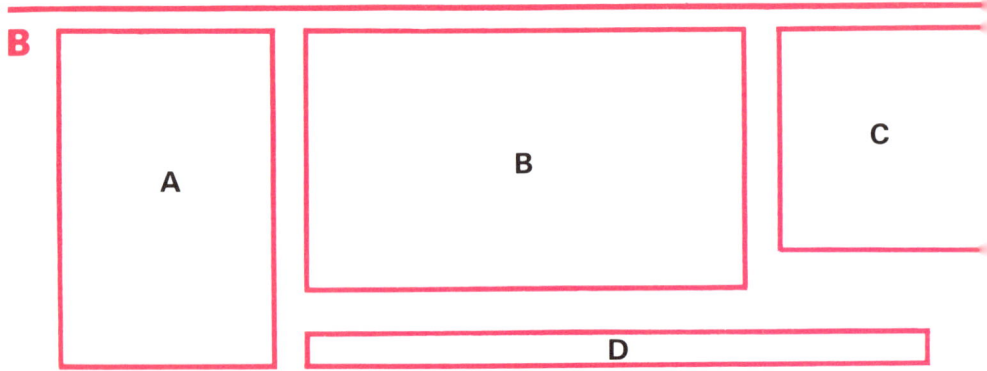

The shapes A, B, C and D have been drawn to the scale 5 mm to 1 cm.
For each shape find
1 the actual length and breadth   **2** the perimeter   **3** the area

C When the length and breadth of a square or rectangle are measured in **metres** (m), the area is measured in **square metres** (m²).

Find the area in m² of each of the following
1 a rectangle 13 m by 7 m   **2** a rectangle 36 m by 8 m.
3 a kitchen floor measuring 7 m long and $4\frac{1}{2}$ m wide
4 the school corridor 28 m in length and 1.5 m in width
5 a square of plaster board each side of which measures $2\frac{1}{2}$ m
6 a roll of paper 18 m long and 50 cm wide
7 a plank of wood 5 m long and 20 cm wide.

D The irregular shape is made up of two rectangles A and B shown by the dotted line.

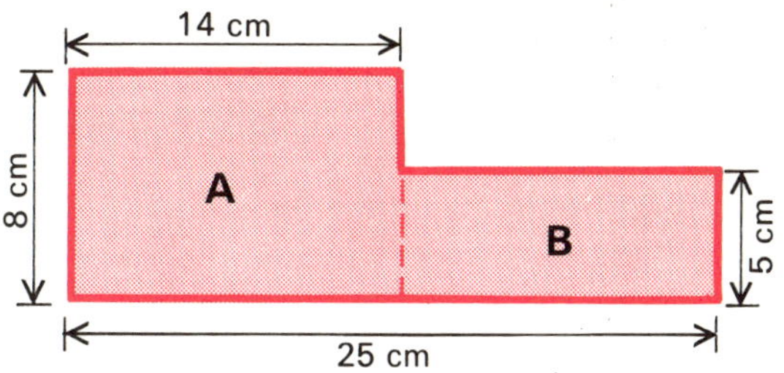

Find in cm² the area of
1 rectangle A   2 rectangle B.
3 What is the area of the irregular shape?
4 Make a rough sketch of the shape and divide it into two rectangles in another way.
5 Find the area of the shape again. Check that the answer agrees with **3**.
6 Find the perimeter of the irregular shape.
7 Using the same method, find the area of each irregular shape M and N.

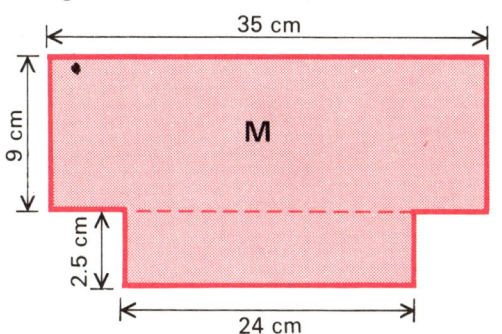

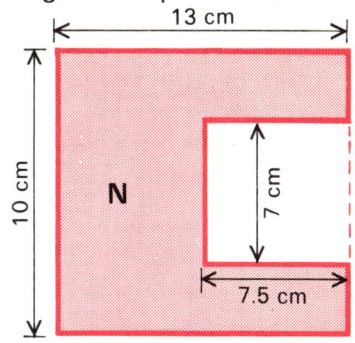

E The surface of shape S is covered with equal square units. 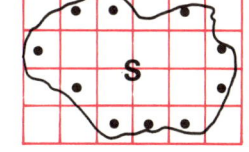
1 Count the whole square units.
2 Count the part square units which are half or more (those marked with a dot).
3 Add the number of whole square units to those which are half or more. The total is the approximate area of the shape in square units.
4 In the same way find, in square units, the approximate area of shapes T, U and V.

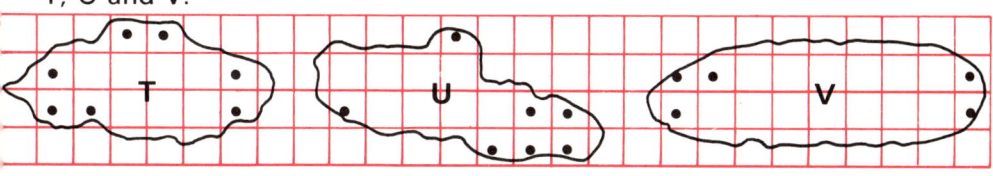

Which shape has   5 the largest area   6 the smallest area?

7 The surface of each of the shapes X and Y is covered with cm². Find the approximate area of each in cm².

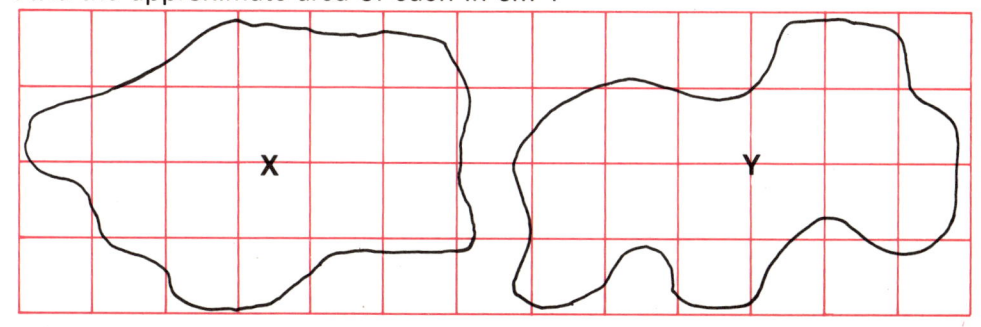

63

UNIT 31

Shapes circles

A First make sure that you can use a pair of compasses correctly.
Practise drawing many circles of different sizes.

Measure in mm the radius of
1. circle E   2. circle F.

Draw circles with a radius
3. twice that of E
4. half that of F.

Draw circles with radii of
5. 3.7 cm   6. 2.3 cm   7. 4.9 cm.

8. Calculate the diameter of each of the circles you have drawn. Check your answers by measuring.

Find the diameter of a circle, the radius of which is
9. 38 mm   10. 2.5 cm   11. 1.6 m   12. 5.8 cm
13. 0.9 cm   14. 67 mm   15. 50 cm   16. 105 mm

17. What do you know about the length of all the radii in the same circle?

B Measure in mm the diameter of
1. circle G   2. circle H.

3. What is the radius of each circle?

4. Draw circles of the same size as G and H.

Draw circles with diameters of
5. 4.6 cm   6. 52 mm   7. 74 mm.

Find the radius of a circle, the diameter of which is
8. 64 mm   9. 4.2 cm   10. 5 m   11. 1.8 cm
12. 3.6 cm   13. $\frac{1}{2}$ m   14. 11.6 cm   15. 114 mm

C

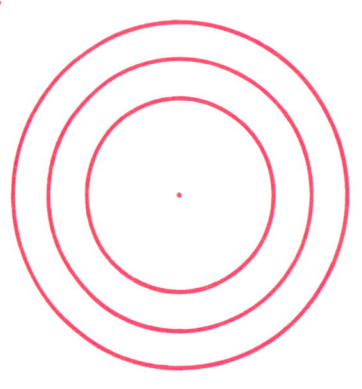

The circles in the drawing have the same centre.
They are called **concentric circles**.

1. Draw a circle of radius 1.8 cm.
2. Draw two concentric circles increasing the radius by 6 mm for each.
3. Write the length of the diameter of each circle.

Write a sentence which describes in any circle
4. a radius   5. a diameter.

6. What is the relationship between the radius and the diameter of the same circle

D

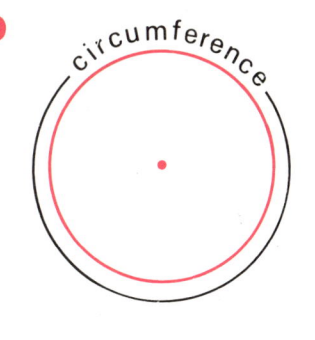

The distance round a circle is called its **circumference.**

1 What is the circumference of a 1 metre trundle wheel in cm?

If the wheel clicks 150 times in measuring a distance, write the distance

2 in metres   **3** in km.

How many times does the trundle wheel turn in going

4 $\frac{1}{2}$ km   **5** 0.1 km   **6** 0.3 km?

The circumference of a wheel measures 40 cm.
Write, first in cm and then in m, the distance the wheel travels in

7 1 turn   **8** 10 turns   **9** 100 turns.

The circumference of a cycle wheel measures 1.5 m.
How many times does the wheel go round in travelling

10 15 m   **11** 30 m   **12** 300 m   **13** 1.5 km?

E

Using compasses and a set square draw the quadrant of a circle the radius of which is   **1** 3.5 cm   **2** 56 mm.

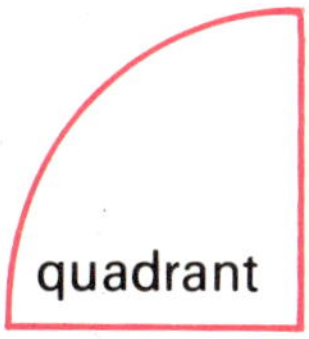

3 How many degrees are there in the angle of the quadrant? Give the reason for your answer.

4 Draw a semi-circle with a diameter of 72 mm.

5 How many degrees are there in the straight angle at the centre?

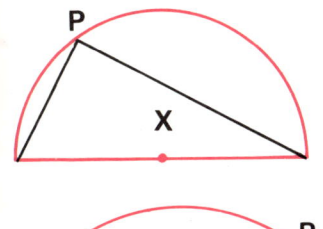

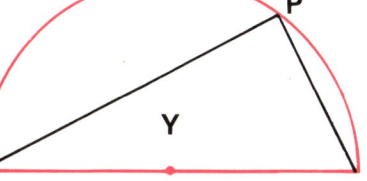

6 Measure in mm the diameter of each semi-circle X and Y. Then draw them.

7 Mark any point P on the circumference of each semi-circle and join it to each end of the diameter.

8 Measure the angle at the circumference using a set square.

9 Mark other points on the circumference and repeat the exercise.

Remember
The angle at the circumference of a semi-circle is always 90°.

Measure
1 the radius of the circle.
2 ∠AOB at the centre of the circle (use a set square). 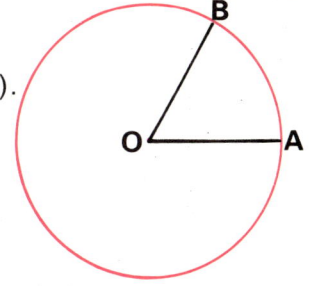
3 Draw the circle and the angle at the centre.
4 With the compasses step off AB round the circumference.
5 Join the points. Name the shape you have drawn inside the circle.
6 Repeat the exercise with an angle of 45° at the centre of the circle.
7 Name the shape you have drawn inside the circle.

65

UNIT 32
Solids   cubes, cuboids   volume

A

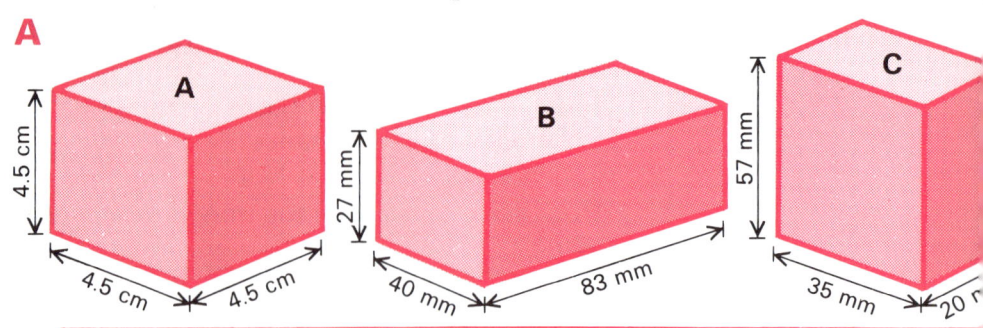

(Box A: 4.5 cm × 4.5 cm × 4.5 cm)
(Box B: 40 mm × 83 mm × 27 mm)
(Box C: 35 mm × 20 mm × 57 mm)

> The drawings show three boxes. These are called **solids**.
> They are also called **3-D shapes** because they each have three dimensions: **length**, **breadth** (width), **height** (thickness).

1 Measure and draw the table below.
Then write in the table the three dimensions of each box in cm in mm

	box A		box B		box C	
	cm	mm	cm	mm	cm	mm
length						
breadth						
height						

How many faces has
2 box A   3 box B   4 box C?

From the measurements on box A write the name of
5 the shape of each face   6 this kind of solid.

From the measurements on boxes B and C write the name of
7 the shape of each face   8 this kind of solid.

B   Write in cm the dimensions of the box
1 the length   2 the width
3 the height.

From the drawing, write the measurements of
4 the top   5 the front
6 the end.

(Box: top, end, front; 36 mm × 40 mm × 64 mm)

Using a set square make a full size drawing of
7 the bottom   8 the back
9 the end you cannot see.
Put the dimensions correctly on each drawing.

10 Name the shape of each of the faces you have drawn.
11 How many pairs of faces on the box have the same dimensions?

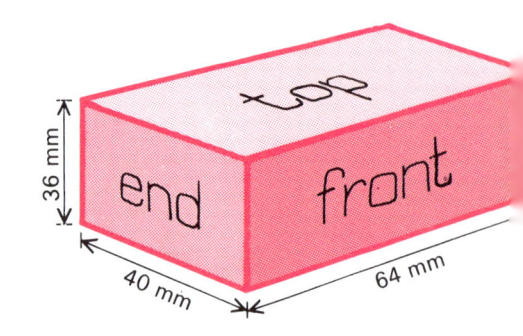

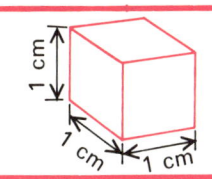

C

The amount of space a solid takes up is called its **volume**.
Volume is measured in cubes.
The drawing shows a centimetre cube (1 cm³).

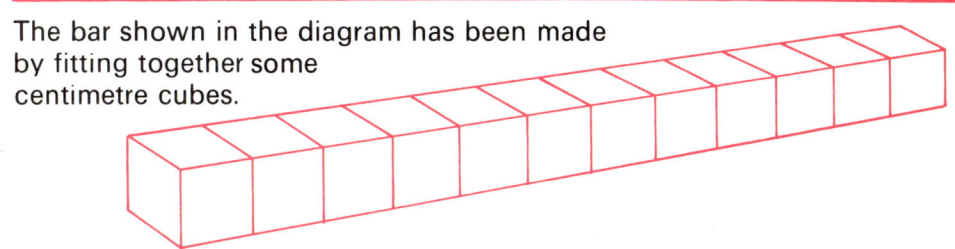

The bar shown in the diagram has been made by fitting together some centimetre cubes.

1. Find, by counting, the number of centimetre cubes needed to make the bar.
2. Write and complete. The volume of the bar is ☐ cm³.
3. What is the length; the breadth; the height of the bar?
4. How many centimetre cubes would be required to make a bar 10 cm long, 1 cm wide and 1 cm high? Write the volume of this bar in cm³.
5. The volume of a wood block is **15 cm³**. If it is 1 cm wide and 1 cm high, how long is it?

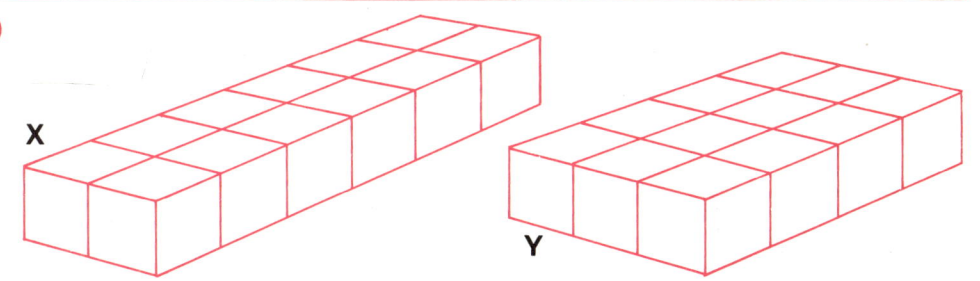

D

The rectangular solid (cuboid) marked X is made by fitting together centimetre cubes.
1. Find its length, width and height.
2. How many centimetre cubes are used to make the cuboid X? Write and complete: The volume of X is ☐ cm³.

The cuboid Y is also made with centimetre cubes.
3. Find its length, width and height.
4. How many centimetre cubes are used to make the cuboid Y? Write and complete: The volume of Y is ☐ cm³.
5. Compare the volume of the bar in **C2** with the volumes of X and Y. What do you discover?

Remember
Different shapes of solids can have the same volume.

Find the area in cm² of the bottom of
6. the bar   7. cuboid X   8. cuboid Y.   What do you discover?

9. Get 18 centimetre cubes.
Make as many cuboids each 1 cm high as you can.
Write the length and width of each cuboid you make.

67

UNIT 33
Looking back

A

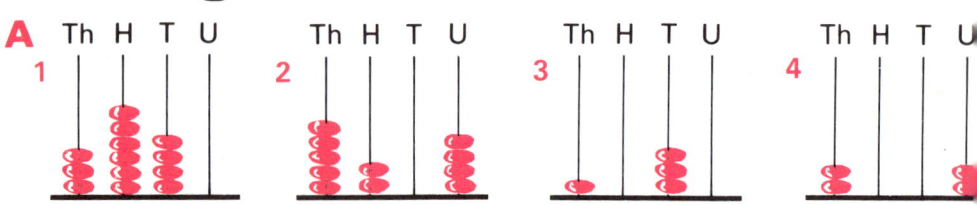

1, 2, 3, 4 (abacus pictures: Th H T U)

Write the number shown on each abacus picture above in figures and then in words.

Write in figures, as a decimal, the number shown on each abacus picture below.

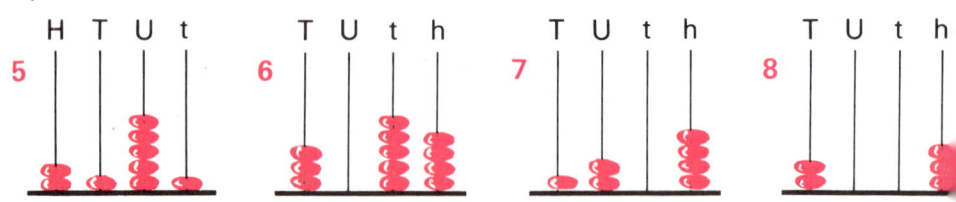

5 (H T U t), 6 (T U t h), 7 (T U t h), 8 (T U t h)

Write the value of the 2 in each of the numbers below.
9 184.25   10 2103.6   11 483.72   12 926.48   13 4261.8   14 192.3

Write as decimals.
15 72 tenths   16 156 hundredths   17 208 tenths
18 309 hundredths   19 6 hundredths   20 51 hundredths

B Multiply by 10.
1 £2·18   2 £5·60   3 £3·09   4 £0·20   5 £10·0
6 2.4 cm   7 0.7 cm   8 4.85 m   9 2.07 m   10 0.04 m

Divide by 10.
11 70 kg   12 5 litres   13 3.5 kg   14 0.7 litres   15 10 cm
16 £6   17 £2·50   18 £0·30   19 £21·40   20 £30·8

Multiply by 100.
21 4 kg   22 0.4 cm   23 0.75 litres   24 0.02 m   25 3.25 k
26 £5·36   27 £2·80   28 £6·63   29 £0·08   30 £0·90

Divide by 100.
31 750 kg   32 2510 litres   33 48 kg   34 20 litres   35 6 m
36 £2577   37 £330   38 £116   39 £70   40 £4

C

1 Name each of the triangles by its angles and then by its sides.

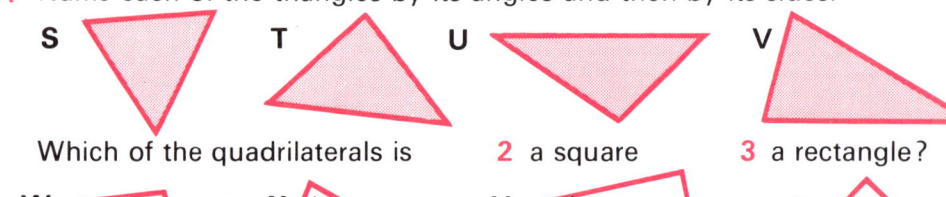

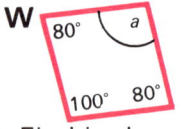

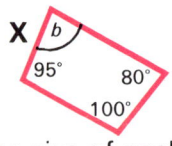

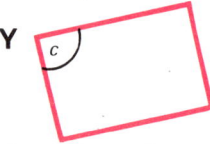

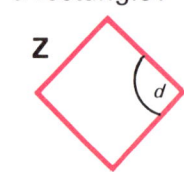

S   T   U   V

Which of the quadrilaterals is   2 a square   3 a rectangle?

W (80°, a, 100°, 80°)   X (b, 95°, 80°, 100°)   Y (c)   Z (d)

4 Find in degrees the size of each angle a, b, c, d.

68

D
1. How many degrees are there in a complete turn?

Write the measurement, in degrees, of each of the angles in the circles below which is 2 shaded ▢ 3 shaded ■.

M   N   O   P   Q   R

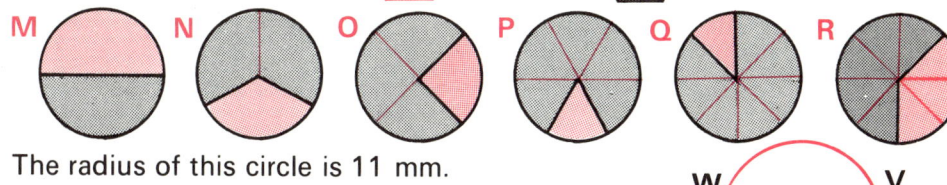

The radius of this circle is 11 mm.
Write the length of the lines
4. UV   5. WX.
6. What is the name given to each of these lines?

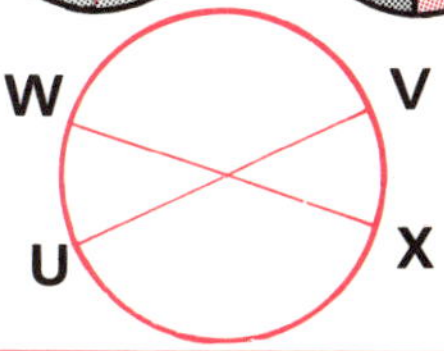

E
1. The diagram shows how 3 girls shared £7·92.
What fraction of the whole one did each girl receive?

Carol   Ann   Julie

2. How much money did each girl receive?

The pie chart was made to show how much the school has saved towards the target of £200.
Target £200
parents, ex-pupils, children

How much has been saved by
3. the parents   4. the children   5. the ex-pupils?
6. How much more money must be saved?

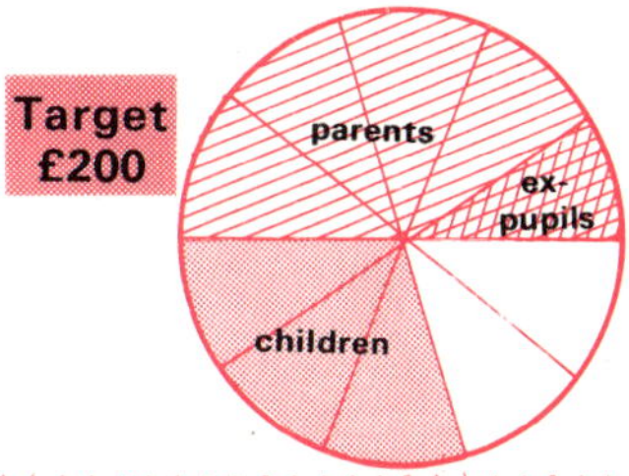

The graph shows the amount saved by each of 4 classes.
7. What does one small division on the horizontal scale represent?
8. How much has each class saved?

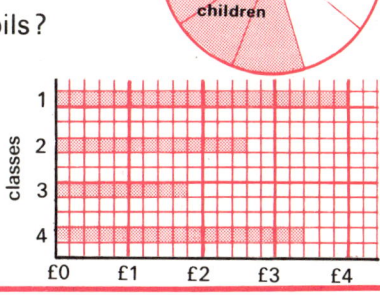

classes 1, 2, 3, 4 — £0 £1 £2 £3 £4

F
1. Draw a circle of 30 mm radius. 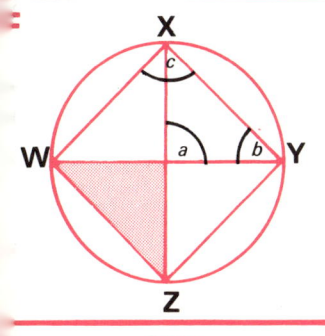
2. Draw two diameters which are perpendicular to one another.
3. Join the ends of the diameters.
4. How many degrees are there in
   angle a   angle b   angle c?

Name the shaded triangle by
5. its angles   6. its sides.

G 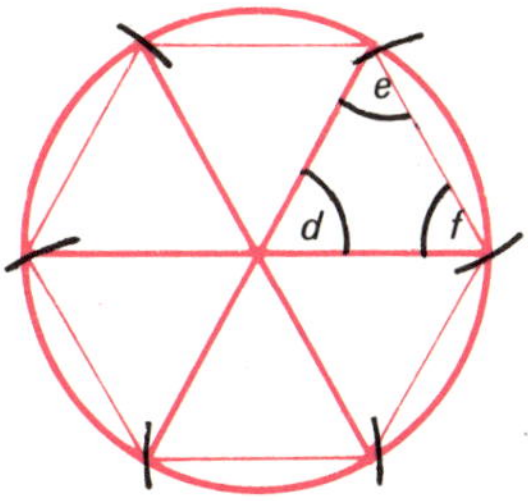
1. Draw a circle of 35 mm radius.
2. Mark off the radius round the circumference.
3. Join the points on the circumference.
4. What is the name of the shape you have drawn in the circle?
5. Join the points on the circumference to the centre.

Name the triangles according to   6. their sides   7. their angles.
8. How many degrees are there in   angle d   angle e   angle f?

69

UNIT 34
Looking back

A How many times can each of the following be filled from the litre measure?
1. measure X
2. measure Y
3. measure Z

How many times can each of the following be filled from the measure X
4. measure Y   5. measure Z?

6. The measures are marked
W 1 litre   X ½ litre   Y 200 mℓ   Z 100 mℓ
Write the capacity of X, Y and Z each as a decimal fraction of a litre.

7. Find, in litres, the total capacity of the four measures.

Write, in mℓ, the capacity represented by one small division on
8. measure W   9. measure X   10. measure Y   11. measure Z

Write the answers to 8–11 as decimal fractions of a litre.

Write the mass in grams of the following quantities of water.

| 1 litre of water has a mass of 1 kg |

12. ½ litre   13. 100 mℓ   14. 250 mℓ   15. 900 mℓ

B Write to the nearest 10p.
1. 37p   2. 72p   3. 65p   4. 46p   5. 83p
6. 18p   7. 21p   8. 59p   9. 35p   10. 99p

Write to the nearest cm.
11. 38 mm   12. 87 mm   13. 14 mm   14. 76 mm   15. 45 mm
16. 6.1 cm   17. 9.9 cm   18. 2.2 cm   19. 5.7 cm   20. 6.8 cm

Write to the nearest £.
21. £8·75   22. £9·50   23. £16·38   24. £13·17   25. £6·90
26. £12·25   27. £18·30   28. £7·60   29. £5·09   30. £10·5

C Write these 12-hour clock times as 24-hour clock times.
1. 7.30 a.m.   2. 10.45 a.m.   3. 11.37 a.m.   4. 10 a.m.   5. midday
6. 1 p.m.   7. 2.20 p.m.   8. 10.25 p.m.   9. 11.18 p.m. 10. midnight

Write these times as 12-hour clock times. Use a.m. or p.m.
11. 07.00   12. 15.15   13. 09.53   14. 17.08   15. 12.34
16. 16.00   17. 01.30   18. 20.05   19. 21.49   20. 23.20

How many minutes from
21. 10.23 a.m. to 11.15 a.m.   22. 8.25 p.m. to 9.10 p.m.
23. 9.29 a.m. to 10.16 a.m.   24. 11.58 a.m. to 12.15 p.m.?

How many hours from
25. 7 a.m. to 11 a.m.   26. 10 a.m. to noon   27. 11 a.m. to 1 p.m.
28. 9 p.m. to 2 a.m.   29. 10.30 a.m. to 12.30 p.m. 30. 12.30 p.m. to 2 p.m.

How many h and min from
31. 2.30 a.m. to 4.05 a.m.   32. 4.15 p.m. to 6.30 p.m.
33. 7.18 a.m. to 11.10 a.m.   34. 11.45 a.m. to 2.10 p.m.
35. 10.17 a.m. to 1.18 p.m.   36. 11.19 p.m. to 3 a.m.?

D Copy and complete the following using +, −, × or ÷ in place of ●

1. 3 ● 6 = 10 ● 8
2. 16 ● 9 = 21 ● 3
3. 3 ● 8 = 20 ● 4
4. 7 ● 9 = 4 ● 4
5. 8 ● 8 = 20 ● 4
6. 12 ● 3 = 4 ● 5
7. 24 ● 8 = 10 ● 7
8. 7 ● 7 = 50 ● 1
9. 9 ● 6 = 34 ● 20
10. 6 ● 4 = 8 ● 3
11. 20 ● 10 = 6 ● 5
12. 63 ● 7 = 15 ● 6

E These coins were collected from four tills at a supermarket.

	£1	FIFTIES	TWENTIES	TENS	FIVES	TWOS	1p
till 1	125	19	20	38	48	59	126
till 2	179	25	25	40	97	101	75
till 3	148	13	34	22	23	75	48
till 4	136	18	58	45	79	80	125

1. Find the total amount from each till.
2. Find the grand total from the four tills.

Find the total amount collected in

3. £s 4. FIFTIES 5. TWENTIES 6. TENS 7. FIVES 8. TWOS 9. 1p.

10. Find the total value of all the coins.
Compare the answers to **2** and **10**. If they do not agree, find the error.

F Look at the prices of radios advertised in each of two shops.

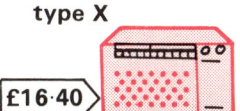

type W £10·80 type X £16·40 type Y £20 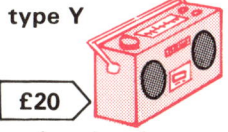 type Z £39·20

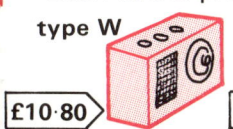

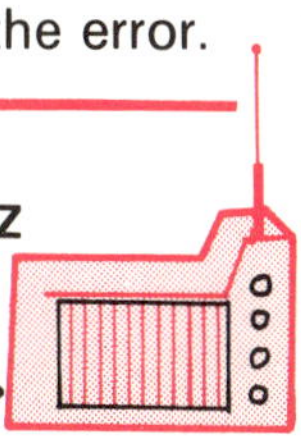

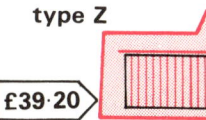

Super Stores offer **one tenth** off each price for a cash sale.
Electra Stores offer **one eighth** off each price for a cash sale.
How much would be saved on each set if bought for cash at

1. Super Stores
2. Electra Stores?

How much would each set cost if bought at the reduced price at

3. Super Stores
4. Electra Stores?

G Use this part of a calendar to find the days of the week for these dates.

FEBRUARY

M	Tu	W	Th	F	S	S
				1	2	3	4
5	6	7	8	9	10	11
12	13	14	15	16	17	18
19	20	21	22	23	24	25
26	27	28				

1. February 6th
2. February 18th
3. January 31st
4. January 1st
5. March 1st
6. March 15th
7. April 1st

Now find the dates for these days.

8. the 1st Sunday in February
9. the 2nd Tuesday in February
10. the 4th Friday in February
11. the 2nd Wednesday in March

H Write the value of each letter in these examples.

1. 13g
  + h75
  ─────
   313

2. 46i
  + 5j8
  ─────
  1000

3. 1x59
  + 16k
  ─────
  1225

4.   onm
  + 999
  ─────
  1111

5. 416
  − q9p
  ─────
   219

6. 50r
  − 1s6
  ─────
   374

7. 835
  − u67
  ─────
   6t8

8. 5w2
  − 333
  ─────
   16v

71

Designed by Peter Sinclair (Design and Print) Ltd, Wetherby
Printed in England by Chorley & Pickersgill Ltd, Leeds